THE WEST HIGHLAND WHITE TERRIER

POPULAR DOGS' BREED SERIES

B. Thurse

Ch. Banner of Branston, 1962

B. Thurs

Ch. Bardel of Branston, 1965

THE WEST HIGHLAND WHITE TERRIER

D. MARY DENNIS

POPULAR DOGS

London

To my husband who all his life has been
a staunch supporter of this lovely breed—
and also to all my dogs who for thirty-
five years have given me so much pleasure

POPULAR DOGS PUBLISHING CO LTD
3 Fitzroy Square, London W1

An imprint of The Hutchinson Publishing Group

London Melbourne Sydney Auckland
Wellington Johannesburg and agencies
throughout the world

First published 1967
Second edition revised 1970
Third edition revised 1973
Fourth edition revised 1976
© D. M. Dennis 1967, 1970, 1973 and 1976

Printed in Great Britain by offset litho by
The Anchor Press Ltd, and bound by
Wm Brendon & Son Ltd, both of Tiptree, Essex

ISBN 0 09 126810 9

CONTENTS

ILLUSTRATIONS

IN THE TEXT

AUTHOR'S INTRODUCTION

My introduction to West Highland White Terriers began when I was but sixteen and first met the boy who was later to become my husband. His father, Nelson F. Dennis, had two or three Westies as early as 1910 and from that time the family were never without one. After the First World War Mr Dennis senior purchased from Mrs Bernard Lucas, Highclere Rose, the winner of three reserve C.C.s, and from this bitch the first West Highland I ever owned was descended. After his father's death in 1921, my husband and his mother kept the dogs in partnership, registering the prefix 'Oughton'. At that time they resided in West Hartlepool, Co. Durham, travelling facilities were not too good, and so their attendance at shows was confined to the north-east of England. In 1923 they moved south into Essex, taking eleven bitches and one dog with them. Shortly afterwards five of the bitches were sold to Miss Errington who, later, was to become better known as Mrs Hewson, the owner of the large and well-known 'Clint' Kennel. Many of the later 'Clints' were descended from the five bitches bought from Mrs Dennis.

In marrying someone who had owned West Highlands from his youth it could have been forecast that I, too, would quickly come to love them as my husband did. I had always been fond of dogs but had never thought seriously of having one as anything other than a pet. Soon after we were married, my mother-in-law told me that the house would never be home without a dog, and as, for her, there was only one breed it would, of course, have to be a West Highland White Terrier. So, when the next litter of puppies arrived, I became the owner of my very first Westie, a bitch we called Judy, whom I remember quite clearly to this day. She was a wonderful character and most intelligent. From her first litter I kept a dog, and it was with him I had my initiation into show business. I do not think he was a very good dog, and I know that I was quite inexperienced in show preparation, but I remember the judge, Mrs D. F. Gardiner, taking the trouble to tell me some of the mistakes I had made in handling my dog and advising me about his good and not so good points. I have never forgotten her kindness to me that day; constructive advice from judges can be so helpful to beginners, and hers had really fired my interest in dog-breeding. I bought a pair of West Highlands from my mother-in-law and from them bred some quite good specimens. By now I was learning fast and well and truly bitten by the show bug. In those days I had little hope of winning anything, except in the most lowly classes. The Wolveys, the Rushmoors, the Clints, the Leals, the Breans, and the Furzefields were in an impregnable position and quite unbeatable. But every dog has his day, and mine was looming on the horizon. In 1939, the war brought everything to a standstill, and my kennel, like so many others, had to be closed down. Deciding how to dispose of about thirty dogs was a heartbreaking task, but I managed to retain ten; eight bitches and two dogs, which had to go to a friend's boarding kennel for the duration. With these ten I had hopes of making a start again in what, at that time, some people thought would be only a year or two. However, by the time it was possible to get a home together again and have what was left of the dogs back— only six of them—they were getting elderly, and only two bitches were fit to breed from. From these two, and Belinda of Branston in particular, the present-day Branstons were revived.

I shall never forget the thrill of breeding my first champion. From that time on other champions followed in fairly quick succession: so many lovely dogs, each wonderful in its own way, but my beloved Ch. Barrister I shall always consider one of the greatest dogs I ever bred. He was a great showman and a wonderful stud dog, siring many champions. But every champion one breeds gives a feeling of satisfaction, and it seems impossible to imagine that a day may come when interest in them will wane.

Dog breeding is hard work. No one can expect to get to the

top by an easy way. The only certain way of knowing dogs is to be able, when necessary, to do every task yourself: staying up all night with a bitch whelping, and seeing to her welfare and comfort; knowing the joy of being the first to handle what you hope may be the best Westie ever bred; enduring the small hours, cold and stiff, when nothing much seems to be happenng; scrubbing out kennels and washing blankets and sacks; preparing innumerable bowls of milk, and scraping raw meat for the baby puppies, especially in winter when you would much rather be indoors by a fire. And this, seven days a week and at Christmas and on other holidays too. If you can do that and keep a cheerful countenance then you love dogs and deserve some reward.

Breeding and showing dogs has always been one of my greatest pleasures, and my husband's. Without his help none of my success would have been possible; it has always been a combined effort. We have travelled thousands of miles together, year in year out, hardly ever missing a show, and enjoying every bit of it. We often talk of the days when we used to set off in a car that was none too reliable. The journey had to be planned almost as a major operation, and it took about twice as long as it would today. But through these travels we made many good friends and met some of the nicest people one could wish to meet, all with the same interest in life, and furtherance of our lovely breed.

Both my husband and I have been judging for a great many years, and in 1964 I had the pleasure of judging a very nice entry at Crufts. In 1969 my husband, G. B. Dennis, judged a very large entry at this most famous of all shows—a task anyone is very honoured to be invited to undertake. I can ask nothing better for anyone than that they should reap as much pleasure and satisfaction from breeding and showing West Highland White Terriers as I do.

It is very satisfactory to report that in 1972 West Highlands still continued to hold the top placings for all the terrier breeds. It is good to know that more and more people appreciate the many fine qualities of the breed—great sturdy little dogs with fine temperaments that appeal to so many people.

In this third edition of the book, five photographs and two new pedigrees have been introduced to keep readers up-to-date with the history of the breed.

I should like to make a special appeal to all breeders and owners of dogs at this time when there is a great deal of suffering among animals for various reasons. So much is just lack of thought and sensitivity to the dog's feelings. To leave a dog shut up for hours or more can cause intense distress. Because of the whimsical vagaries of railways or airlines, dogs have been known to arrive in a collapsed, or at the least very distressed state at the end of a long journey and I feel sure that the genuine dog lover will take any and every step to see to the welfare of animals subjected to the ordeal of travel.

It was with great pleasure that in 1973 I accepted the invitation to judge Westies at the Californian Terrier Show, where so many exhibits were beautifully presented. Some I found overweight and larger than is customary here, but such an array of champions was overwhelming. Yet I found my top winners from the more junior ranks. I counted it a great privilege to handle and admire them.

In 1974 I had a most pleasant visit to Sweden where I judged the West Highland White Terrier Club Show in Stockholm. The breed has made great progress there in the last few years and I was delighted to find so many good ones. The Swedish are so enthusiastic and their frequent visits to the major shows in this country are manifestly worthwhile as they are almost as conversant with the breeding and performance of the exhibits here as at home. The Swedish people, after those of Great Britain and the USA have, I think, done more than most to increase the popularity of the breed.

As this edition goes to press, I should also like to record one of the greatest moments of my career in dogs. On 1 November 1975 I judged the combined West Highland White Terrier Clubs' Show at Wakefield with a near record entry of 210, with 130 exhibits. The quality of all was so high, and winning dogs and bitches were so excellent, that I feel I can never again hope to see their equal. Ch. Glengordon Hannah is as near perfect as anyone could wish, but still had to give place to Ch. Glenalwine Sunny Boy who is a real aristocrat. This was a day I shall remember for the rest of my life.

And now I must express my appreciation to those who have written to me from all over the world about this book. I am very glad to know that so many people who, like my husband and myself, love the Westie have found it helpful. In this fourth edition I have made some minor additions to the text, brought the appendices up to date again, and replaced four more photographs.

Clacton-on-Sea   D.M.D.
Essex, 1976

I

Origin and Development

THE West Highland White Terrier has attained a degree of popularity that could never have been visualised when the first clubs were formed in Scotland and England in 1905, when, according to many writers on the breed, the little white dogs were beginning to be picked out from the small mixed terriers that had abounded as working dogs in the Scottish Highlands for some three hundred years. It would seem that the breed was first classified at the annual show of The Scottish Kennel Club held at Waverley Market, Edinburgh, 26th to 28th October 1904, the following being a copy of a letter sent by the Secretary of the Scottish Kennel Club to Mr J. A. Urquhart of Rothesay.

'My Dear Sir,
    'I have been requested to provide a short classification for West Highland or Poltalloch Terriers and to ask if you would agree to judge them. The gentleman who makes the request is a specialist in this particular line and does not approve of the Scottish type of these Terriers. He says they should be judged from the working point of view. He says they are the old stock from which the Show Skye has been developed but are not to be judged by the length of the coat, that would be in their way for working. They should have black noses and their weight not over 18 lbs for dogs or 16 lbs for bitches. He says that as to general shape it should make for activity, and the heads and necks for biting and fighting. He also says "the general type would be evident at a glance". I hope you can see your way to judge the variety and I shall be glad to hear from you.
                                    'Yours faithfully,
                                        'A. P. Simpson.'

The ancestors of the breed were in the past known under various names such as Poltalloch, Roseneath, White Scottish, Cairn and Little Skye, and in about 1904 all these were merged to become known as West Highland White Terriers. (The Cairn Terrier was given a separate register and Championship status in 1912.)

I am indebted to the Secretary of The Kennel Club for the following article which appeared in *The Dog Owners Annual*, Canine Literature 1892.

THE POLTALLOCH TERRIER

'A white variety of the Scottish Terrier existed at one time (and stray specimens may exist) under the cognomen of Poltalloch Terriers, and Captain Mackie, who went expressly to Poltalloch to see this variety, describes it as follows:

' "The Poltalloch Terrier weighs from sixteen to twenty pounds, has a determined, vermin destroying look about it, it is well knit together, is a sort of linty white in colour. The hair is hard and bristly, and will be from an inch to two-and-a-half inches in length, excepting on the face and head where it is short, hard and wiry.

' "The body is a medium between cobby and long, but is very deep and stands upon short bony legs, the fore ones nearly straight. Head very long; nose broad and often flesh coloured; teeth extremely large for such a small dog; ears small, prick, and covered with a velvety coat. The tail is slightly bent and carried gaily.

' "I have had the breed and hope to have it again. I know exactly what these dogs are fit for, and may add that no water was ever too cold and that no earth was ever too deep for them."

'A dog answering the above description is in the possession of Mr M'Gavin the Laird of Balumbie and comes to Dundee with him regularly. The ears of Mr M'Gavin's dog are tipped with black, the head and body being a light creamy colour.'

'The Dog Owners Supplement' to the *Bazaar*, dated 27th November 1899, included the following article on Roseneath

Roseneath or White Scottish Terriers, 1899

Colonel Malcolm with his Poltallock Terriers, *c.* 1905

Thomas Fall

Ch. Calluna Ruairidh, 1937

Thomas Fal

Mrs C. Pacey, 1935, with Ch. Wolvey Pintail, Ch. Wolvey Wings,
Ch. Wolvey Prefect, Ch. Wolvey Poacher and Ch. Wolvey Peacock

of Poltalloch. At the beginning of the present century in
Cassel's *New Book of the Dog*, published about 1911 by Robert
Leighton, Col. Malcolm wrote and I quote—

'I have been asked to give an account of these dogs because
I ventured to show them some years ago and to bring before
the general public the claims of this most ancient race. When
I first showed in Edinburgh an old gentleman came up to me
and thanked me most warmly for having revived in his breast
the joys of fifty years before when he used to hunt otters on
the shores of Loch Fyne with Terriers just like mine, colour and
all. I can answer personally for their having been at Poltalloch
sixty years ago, and so they were first known as Poltalloch
Terriers.

'When public attention had been called to them, as I cared
for the breed only and had no ambition to be known as a doggy
man, I joined with a few of those interested in the breed to
form a Club for the promotion of the interests of the West
Highland White Terrier.

'It is still to be found all along the West Coast of Scotland.
I myself have seen good specimens belonging to Ross-shire,
to Skye, and at Ballachulish on Loch Leven, so that it is a breed
with a long pedigree and not an invented breed of the present
day, so I thought it right to disassociate it from the name of
Poltalloch.

'The West Highland Terrier of the old sort—I do not of
course speak of bench dogs—earn their living following fox,
badger and otter wherever they went underground, between,
over, or under rocks that no man could get at to move and
some of such size that a hundred men could not move them
(and Oh! the beauty of their note when they came across the
right scent). I want my readers to understand this and not to
think of a highland fox cairn as if it was an English fox earth
dug in sand; nor of badger work as if it was a question of
locating the badger and digging him out. No, the badger
makes his home among rocks, the smaller ones weighing perhaps two or three tons and probably he has his "hinner end"
against one of three or four hundred tons—no digging him out
—and moreover the passages between the rocks must be taken

as they are; no scratching them a little wider. So if your dog's ribs are a trifle too big he may crush (squeeze) one or two through the narrow slit and then stick. He will never be able to pull himself back—at least not until starvation has so reduced him that he will probably, if set free, be unable to win (as we say in Scotland) his way back to the open.

'I remember a tale of one of my father's keeper's terriers who got so lost the keepers went daily to the cairn hoping against hope. At last one day a pair of bright eyes were seen at the bottom of a hole. They did not disappear when the dog's name was called; a brilliant idea seized one of the keepers, the dog evidently could not get up, so a rabbit-skin was folded into a small parcel round a stone and let down on a string. The dog at once seized the situation and the skin, held on and was drawn up, and fainted on reaching the mouth of the hole. He was carried home, nursed and recovered.'

This illustrates the intelligence of the West Highland of bygone days. It is still evident today although few of them get the opportunity of displaying their working qualities. The writer was recently informed that one of the famous Hunts still uses a West Highland Terrier in preference to any other breed for bolting foxes. In the West Country they are regularly used as working dogs and are sent on their own without human assistance to fetch up the herd of milking cows from the pastures.

Mr Holland Buckley senior, a very early authority on West Highland White Terriers, recorded in his book on the breed, in 1911, that he had seen papers at Versailles and pictures, bearing the imprint of the time of Louis The Great, that were identical with the modern West Highland except that some were prick-eared and others drop-eared or semi-erect.

There are, of course, the two famous paintings by Sir Edward Landseer, R.A., of about 1839, 'Sporting Dogs' and 'Dignity and Impudence', both of which include a West Highland White Terrier.

Many romantic stories are told of their early days, among which is the famous request of James the First of England, in the early seventeenth century, to send to Argyllshire for six little white 'earth dogs' to be forwarded as a present to the King of France. It is certain that he must have placed much value on them because he gave specific instructions that they should be sent in two ships lest one should be lost on route. A letter from India was recently received by the Author stating that the ships of the Spanish Armada carried small white dogs of West Highland type to catch the rats on the ships. History has recorded that after a disastrous naval battle in the late sixteenth century, several of the galleons were driven northwards, where most of them were wrecked on the coasts of the Western Isles of Scotland. If this is true it may account for the little white dogs of Scotland being found in Spanish ships. In fact, Mr Holland Buckley states in his book that, 'Col. Malcolm of Poltalloch claimed by an attenuated chain of reasoning (which although picturesque and vivid, scarcely carried conviction to the student) that the Scottish Terrier owed its existing type to the influence of outside blood and that the original terrier was actually of the type of the West Highlander.' If Col. Malcolm was right, perhaps the outside blood came from Spain. That the original West Highland Terrier was bred for its working and sporting qualities has been firmly established. Their intelligence is very much above average and they are really clever schemers when it comes to worrying vermin out of their holes, and their tenacity of purpose invariably means there is only one end to their work.

Mrs Lionel Portman, in 1910, wrote an article in *The Field* about the happy days spent hunting badger with a team of West Highland Terriers, and the same dogs were exhibited with considerable success. Mrs Portman prefaces her article with: 'Badger digging is, undoubtedly, the supreme test of a working terrier. Rabbiting improves his nose and condition. Ratting combines business with pleasure. But to find a badger deep in the labyrinths of a large earth, and to stick to him, possibly for hours together, baying and sniffing at him so that he has no time to dig—a thing he can do much faster than two men—is a task requiring perseverance, grit and stamina of the highest order. As we feel these qualities are worth, at least as much encouragement as show points, we invariably enter all our terriers to badger soon after they have received their preliminary training.'

The foregoing will give the reader some idea of the hard work put in by the old stalwarts on the several regional types to develop them into a single breed, and the controversy that must have existed over the selection of a name to suit all regions. It is quite possible, although there is no evidence to prove it, that the present name was a compromise to include all the white dogs of the West Highlands, hence the name, the West Highland White Terrier.

Show Development

The earlier part of this chapter has given a brief outline of the early West Highland White Terrier under its various aliases as a working terrier, and I now propose to chronicle its evolution into a show dog.

At a show held in Birmingham, in 1860, classes for 'Scotch Terriers' were included. It appears to have been the first time any terriers were classified, and a 'White Skye' was among the winners. The first show held in Scotland was at Glasgow in 1871, and here again 'Scottish Terriers' were classified, but I can find no record of the winners, and the term probably covered all the short-legged terriers of Scotland.

A White Scottish Terrier puppy by White Victor out of White Heather (it does not appear to have had a name) was shown by Lady A. Forbes at the 1899 Crystal Palace Show, and was among the winners. At the same show, also, Dr Flaxman showed a team of Roseneath Terriers. The first show where West Highland White Terriers were separately classified was at the Annual Show of the Scottish Kennel Club held at Waverley Market, Edinburgh, 26th to 28th October 1904.

At the next Scottish Kennel Club Show, held in October 1905, Morven won the Championship Certificate at the age of seven-and-a-half months, and in 1907 became the first Champion in the breed. Morven was born 28th March 1905, by Brogach out of Callaig, and was owned by Mr Colin Young of Fort William. Brogach has been described in some books as being a biggish terrier with great bone and substance generally, yet

weighing only 17 lb. I can find no record of the weight of
Morven, who was stated to be smaller than his sire. It is also
recorded that Athol, reputed to have been Morven's best son,
weighed 16 lb, and Ch. Glenmohr Model, the son of Athol,
also weighed 16 lb.

Also in 1907, Ch. Cromar Snowflake, by Morven out of
Snowdrift, and Ch. Oronsay, by Conas out of Jean, both
gained their titles and were owned by the Countess of Aberdeen.

The first three Champions were therefore produced in 1907,
and these together with their contemporaries laid the foundation of the breed. In this same year, also, 141 dogs and bitches
were registered.

Between 1907 and 1916 the total registrations of West
Highland dogs and bitches amounted to 3,947, and 27 Cham-
pions were made up. The names of their owners, among others
Miss Viccars (Childwick), Mrs M. A. Logan, Mr Holland
Buckley and his daughter Miss W. Buckley, and their 'Scotia',
Mrs Lionel Portman, Mr C. Clare, Mrs B. Lucas of Highclere
fame, and Mr John Lee, have now become legendary.

Among other breeders and exhibitors during this period
were Mr E. Mullard who was known to many of the present-
day exhibitors as a judge in the 1950s, and, of course, the
famous Mrs C. Pacey who, in the fifty-odd years until her death
in 1963, did more for the breed than anyone else and possibly
more than anyone will ever do. She became one of the best, if
not the best, all round judge in the world and officiated on
every continent and in practically every country where dog
shows were held, and was very much in demand. In her book,
Mrs Pacey says that she made a start and won a lot of awards
with a dog called Wolvey MacNab, born 28th June 1911, by
Athol out of Weddington Sanna, and bred by Mrs H. Shawe.
The first of the many (58) Wolvey Champions was seen in 1916
in Ch. Wolvey Piper, born 24th July 1914 by Ensay out of
Culloch and bred by Mrs S. McLeod on the Isle of Skye,
followed in the same year by Ch. Wolvey Rhoda.

The West Highland White Terrier classes at the Kennel Club
Championship Show in October 1913 are reproduced in
Appendix IV. These should be of great interest to the reader

especially where the prices of the several dogs offered for sale are shown.

After 1916, all shows were stopped by the war. Breeding was prohibited in 1917 and 1918 and no dogs born during this period, except under licence, were allowed to be registered. Due to very stringent food rationing many dogs had to be destroyed, some kennels never started again, and those that were able to keep one or two dogs alive on any food they could get, were in a good position to make a slow start once the restrictions were lifted.

Breeding started once again in 1919, and during that year 126 dogs were registered. The following year shows restarted, registrations increased to 244, and five Champions were made: Mr C. Viccars's Charming of Childwick, Mrs B. Lucas's Highclere Rhalet and Highclere Romp, Mr J. H. Railton's White Sylph, and Mrs C. Pacey's Wolvey Skylark. Registrations increased to 758 in 1925, the highest pre-Second World War total, and remained fairly static until 1928, then declining to around the 600 mark during the economic crisis of the early 1930s, increasing in 1936 to 757. In 1941 they reached their lowest since 1919. Except for the years 1951 to 1954 there has been annual increases, culminating with a record total in 1965 of 3,113.

The years 1920–39 saw 125 Champions being made up and of these 32 were Wolveys, approximately 25 per cent, quite a record.

A complete list of all Champions will be found in Appendix II. It is possible to take note of only a few of these Champions. (The date the dog obtained its title is shown in brackets after the name.)

Mrs Pacey's Ch. Wolvey Patrician who won many Best in Shows and would appear in an extended pedigree of most of today's dogs, was the sire of International Ch. Ray of Rushmoor, Ch. Rodrick of Rushmoor, both owned by Miss V. M. Smith-Wood, Miss P. Pacey's Ch. Wings, Mrs Hewson's Clint Crofter who, although never becoming a Champion was the sire of many outstanding dogs, including Ch. Clint Cocktail (1931), probably the best of the Clints.

Mrs Innes's Ch. Brean Glunyieman (1934) was an outstanding dog, considered by many to be the best of all the Breans.

Mrs Pacey's Ch. Wolvey Pintail (1936) was to my mind the best Wolvey I ever saw, a perfect model and the ideal West Highland Terrier. The way she showed, always to perfection, must have gladdened the hearts of all who saw her. The impression she made on me at that time has remained with me all the years of seeing and showing wonderful dogs. She won Best in Show at the Great Joint Terrier Show in 1936 and, on the following day, at the L.K.A. Show was best bitch.

Miss A. A. Wright's Ch. Calluna Ruairidh (1937), sired by Ch. Ray of Rushmoor, was sire of Miss Turnbull's Ch. Leal Flurry (1938), who was the sire of Mr Hewson's Ch. Melbourne Mathias (1939). Miss Turnbull's Ch. Leal Sterling (1938) was the outstanding dog of that year.

We have a direct line from the bitch Ch. White Sylph (1920) to Ch. Wolvey Guy (1924): Ch. Wolvey Patrician—Int. Ch. Ray of Rushmoor—Ch. Calluna Ruairidh—Ch. Leal Flurry to Ch. Melbourne Mathias and, missing one generation, to his grandson Furzefield Piper, who became a prominent sire when breeding and showing restarted in 1946.

With the advent of the Second World War in 1939 all showing ceased, but this time breeding was not banned, and food was available although difficult to get. Nevertheless, it allowed a few kennels to keep going in a small way, and during the period 1940–42 the yearly registrations averaged approximately 150, increasing to 277 in 1943 and to nearly 500 in 1944, rising steadily, except for a drop of 200 in 1953 (crisis again), until in 1964 they reached the total of 2,884, nearly 100 per cent above the 1958 figure.

At the outbreak of the War—I then kept Cairns as well—all the Cairns and some of the West Highlands were given away and eight bitches were put into boarding kennels and remained there until 1943. I kept the two male dogs with me but, later, one of the dogs joined the bitches in the kennels.

In 1943 circumstances made it possible for me to get the bitches back. I intended to restart breeding in a small way, and nature made certain that it was in a very small way as only two of the bitches ever had any puppies again. One had one litter and the other three litters, but this was a new start. It was from this latter bitch, Belinda of Branston, born 27th December 1937 by Ch. Clint Constable (1936) out of Clint Coacla, that the present-day Branstons were developed. Belinda's first two litters were by Bobby of Branston and Ch. Clint Cyrus (1937) out of Blossom of Chemstone, and the last by Mrs Beel's Freshney Andy by Ch. Melbourne Mathias out of Freshney Crysta, which produced Ch. Binnie of Branston (1949).

Championship shows were permitted again in 1946, but only as Breed Specialist Shows, and after a lapse of six dreary war-ridden years what a tonic it was to have them again. The West Highland White Terrier Club of England held its first show at Peterborough on 11th July of that year, and was greeted with a record entry of 225. To Mrs Winnie Barber fell the honour of awarding the first post-war certificates in the breed. This show was to be memorable for some of the exhibitors: The Hon. Torfrida Rollo won her first certificate with Timochenko of the Roe by Irish Ch. Tam O' Shanter of the Roe, out of Whisper of the Roe. Timochenko gained his full title in 1947. The bitch certificate went to Mr Charles Drake's Macairns Jemima by Ch. Leal Sterling out of Macairns Jeanne, and this was Mr Drake's first Championship Show, his bitch gaining her full title in 1948.

The West Highland White Terrier Club held its first show in Edinburgh on the following August the 11th, with Miss M. Turnbull as judge, and awarded the dog certificate to Mrs Beel's Freshney Andy by Ch. Melbourne Mathias out of Freshney Crysta who, except for his tragic death a month later, would have been a certain champion and also a very dominant sire, for during his short time at stud he sired six champions, including Ch. Cruben Crystal (1948), Ch. Athos of Whitehills (1949) and Ch. Binnie of Branston (1949).

The 'of England' Club held its second show on 28th November 1946, with Mrs Thornton as judge. The dog certificate was awarded to Mrs Pacey's Wolvey Prospect by Ch. Wolvey Prefect (1936) out of Wolvey Poise, and the bitch certificate to Miss E. E. Wade's Freshney Fiametta, by Ch.

Melbourne Mathias out of Freshney Felicia, which in 1947
became the first post-war Champion in the breed, going Best
in Show at the all breeds Championship Show held at Cam-
bridge 10th July 1947, and the winner of six challenge certificates and six best of breeds. Fiametta was a glorious bitch—
although some people considered her too big for a bitch—well
balanced, with charm and character which were brought out to
perfection by her handler, Arthur Wade, who was one of the
greatest professional handlers in Great Britain. Although handling many terriers his great loves were West Highlands and
Sealyhams, and his knowledge of both breeds was almost un-
surpassed. He had a genuine love for all dogs, and many new
exhibitors owed much to his readiness to pass on the vast
knowledge he had gained during his lifetime of work with
them. In his younger days he managed the famous Childwick
Kennels of Miss Viccars.

The beginning of general all-breed Championship Shows
was 1947, the first being held at Peterborough by the East of
England Ladies Kennel Society on 29th–30th May. Here the
dog certificate went to another new breeder, Mrs Finch.
Shiningcliff Simon by Ch. Leal Flurry out of Walney Thistle
gained his title at Leicester the same year, but the greatest
achievement for Simon and his owner was still to come, for at
Crufts in 1950 he was Best Terrier in Show, and in the following month at the Scottish Kennel Club Show at Glasgow he
was awarded Best in Show all Breeds. He was the sire of
several champions. It was a great loss to the breed when Mrs
Finch gave up breeding in about 1955.

It is not proposed to detail all the championship shows since
1947, the few mentioned above being intended to give the
reader some insight into the efforts that were made to re-start
breeding after the Second World War and to prove to the new
exhibitor that if they have the right dog it can win.

During the early period of the post-war years the quality of
the dogs was very high, which may have arisen because during
the war years, although so many of the cream of the fancy
were sent to America and other places abroad, a few of the
most devoted followers of the breed overcame almost insur-

mountable difficulties to keep two or three good brood bitches as a future foundation. The breed was also fortunate in having the services of the last pre-war Ch. Melbourne Mathias, now owned by Mrs McKinney. He was the grand sire of Furzefield Piper from whom so many of today's dogs are descended, as family tree 'B' so clearly illustrates. This 'tree' does not include all the champions sired by the several dogs, but only some of the main branches, but it should be noted that earlier in this chapter I showed how Ch. Melbourne Mathias was directly descended through champions from Ch. White Sylph in 1920.

There is no doubt that Furzefield Piper was the leading stud dog at this time—Piper was a grand dog although a somewhat fiery showman—and would have become a champion except for being penalised for having lost some teeth in a kennel fight. He was the sire of nine champions of whom the most notable was Ch. Hookwood Mentor owned by Miss E. E. Wade who, in turn, sired eleven champions. His greatest son is generally recognised as being my Ch. Barrister of Branston, who also sired eleven champions, and several with two certificates.

Since the resumption of championship shows in 1946, 168 champions have been made up to the end of 1964, and it is obviously not possible to review the merits of all the glorious dogs who have won their titles (a complete list is in Appendix II). I have, however, selected a few who have left their mark on the breed in one way or other.

My Ch. Baffle of Branston, by Freshney Frinton out of Baroness of Branston, is mentioned here as she was the first of the many Branston champions and is still remembered by some who saw her in the ring, a grand-daughter of Ch. Melbourne Mathias.

Mr A. H. Salsbury's Ch. Macconachie Tiena Joy, by Ch. Shiningcliff Simon out of Macconachie Pearlie, well-named, was a very beautiful bitch and the winner of twelve challenge certificates—still a record.

My Ch. Barrister of Branston, by Ch. Hookwood Mentor out of Bloom of Branston, through his eleven champion sons and daughters and several near champions has undoubtedly left his mark on the breed.

Dr and Mrs Russel's Int. Ch. Cruben Dextor, by Ch. Hook-wood Mentor out of Amer. Ch. Cruben Melphis Chloe, quickly gained his title and went to America where he continued his winning ways with many Best in Shows. He has sired more champions in America than any other dog.

Mrs Allom's Ch. Furzefield Pilgrim, by Furzefield Piper out of Furzefield Purpose, is the sire of several champions, including Ch. Wolvey Pied Piper.

Mrs Beel's Ch. Calluna the Poacher, by Calluna Bingo out of Calluna Vermintrude, born 1952, died 1965, was winner of ten challenge certificates and ten best in breeds in just under a year, a record that will take a lot of surpassing. He sired five English champions and several in America, including a complete litter of four.

The Hon. Torfrida Rollo's and, later, Mrs K. Sanson's Ch. Eoghan of Kendrum, by Ch. Barrister of Branston out of Ch. Isla of Kendrum, was sire of several champions, including Ch. Quakertown Questionaire.

Miss Cook's Int. Ch. Famecheck Viking, by Ch. Calluna the Poacher out of Famecheck Fluster, a daughter of Ch. Barrister of Branston exported to America and reputed to have won more Groups and Best of Shows than any other West Highland, was still being shown when ten years old.

Mrs E. A. Green's Ch. Nice Fella of Wynsolot, by Fan Mail of Wynsolot out of Shiningcliff Star Turn, gained fame when winning Reserve Best Terrier at Crufts in 1956. He was a very useful stud, and sired Ch. Banessa of Branston and Ch. Sollershot Sun-up.

My Ch. Banker of Branston, by Ch. Barrister of Branston out of Binty of Branston, sired six champions, the most famous being Ch. Bandsman of Branston and Amer. Ch. Rainsborowe Redvers, now owned by Mrs Barbara Sayers, and the winner of many Best in Shows.

Mrs Kenny Taylor's Ch. Sollershot Sun-up, by Ch. Nice Fella of Wynsolot out of Cotsmoor Crack O' Dawn, sired five champions, including Eng. and Aust. Ch. Busybody of Branston, out of Ch. Brindie of Branston, and Mrs Estcourt's Ch. Citrus Lochinvar of Estcoss. Mrs Pacey's Ch. Wolvey Pied

Piper, by Ch. Furzefield Pilgrim out of Wolvey Padella, was the sire of four champions.

My Ch. Bavena of Branston, by Ch. Banker of Branston out of Famecheck Teresa, was winner of the Terrier Group at Birmingham National and Hove Shows. Exported to Mrs R. K. Mellon, she soon gained her American title.

Miss Cook's Ch. Famecheck Gay Buccaneer, by Ch. Famecheck Gay Crusader out of Ch. Famecheck Lucky Mascot, is probably the most outstanding of all the Famecheck champions.

My Ch. Bandsman of Branston, by Ch. Banker of Branston out of Ch. Banessa of Branston, winner of seven consecutive challenge certificates and Best of Breeds in three months, was reserve Best Terrier at Windsor Championship Show in 1960. He was sire of three champions and several other certificate winners.

Mr and Mrs Granville Ellis's Ch. Slitrig Shining Star of Lynwood, by Ch. Famecheck Gay Buccaneer out of Slitrig Sweet Suzette, was one of a long line of Lynwood champions and a magnificent bitch.

Mrs Kenney Taylor's Ch. Sollershot Soloist, by Ch. Bandsman of Branston out of Citrus Silhouette, was winner of twelve challenge certificates. It was a very great loss to the breed when, in 1965, Mrs Kenney Taylor, owing to domestic reasons had to give up breeding and exhibiting, and her Kennel was disbanded.

Mrs K. Sanson's Ch. Quakertown Quistador, by Ch. Alpin of Kendrum out of Quakertown Querida, was an outstanding dog and an exceptional showman, winner of twelve certificates, Terrier Groups and Best in Shows. He should be a very great influence on the breed.

Among the many other experienced breeders and exhibitors are: Mrs P. Welch from Worcestershire (Glengyle) who although only keeping a fairly small kennel always manages to show something good, and so far has made four champions; Mrs J. Sinclair (Miss Herbert) from Galashiels (Glenalwynne), President of the West Highland Terrier Club (Scotland), who is a very dedicated breeder and exhibitor but unfortunately prevented from showing during the summer months because of business commitments; Mr and Mrs Billy Thompson, from Lancashire (Waideshouse), who have made three champions in their comparatively short time in the breed; Mrs B. Graham, in partnership with her mother Mrs G. Hazel, is a great supporter of the breed; her first champion was Lasara Lee in 1963, and she has also exported several dogs to Scandinavia where they have very quickly gained their local titles; Mrs Sylvia Kearsey, from Warwickshire (Pillerton), one of our younger enthusiasts who in a very short space of time has bred an excellent type. Her first champion was Ch. Pillerton Pippa who was Best of Breed at Crufts 1965. In the West country Mrs J. Beer (Whitebriar) produces stock of high quality, some of the best having made their mark in Canada and the U.S.A. The Citrus kennel, owned by Mr and Mrs G. Lemon, has produced two champions.

The popularity of the West Highland White Terrier has, during the past few years, increased by leaps and bounds, and new names are constantly before us—such as Miss Sheilah Cleland (Birkfell) who by her devotion to the female of the species has bred three bitch champions. Mr and Mrs Bertram have made three lovely champions in a short space of time and no doubt more will be heard of the Highstile prefix in the future. Miss Fisher (Lindenhall) has an excellent type and has bred two champions, one of which is owned by Mrs Millen who really had the traditional beginner's luck by making her first Westie a champion. The Alpinegay prefix first became well known when Mrs Wheeler made Impressario a champion and later exported him to Mrs Church in America where he had instant success. A year later, in 1968, his younger brother, Alpinegay Sonata, gained his title in the capable hands of Miss K. Owen. There are many others, like Mrs Muriel Coy (Cedarfells) with two champions, and Mrs Pratten whose Rainsborowe prefix occurs in many of the pedigrees of recent winners, while from Scotland come such well known names as Mr C. Berry (Incheril), Mr W. Stevenson (Parkendot), and Mr and Mrs Gellan (Backmuir).

In 1965 it was on record that West Highlands had maintained their position of second in the Terrier group but this has now been surpassed and they head the group with a record registration of 4,160 in 1968. It must be hoped for the good of the breed that, as the numbers increase, standards are not allowed to fall, and that the same carefully thought-out breeding programmes which prevailed in the past will still be followed by the great majority of breeders.

The unprecedented demand for top class show stock from this country in 1972 is incredible and very complimentary as it proves that the large majority of exports are well up to standard and that there are a lot of very satisfied clients who expect and get what they pay for.

In 1974 the number of registrations was 4630. This number has only twice before been surpassed with 4837 in 1969 and 4933 in 1970. It would seem that the economic problems are not sufficient to deter either newcomers or veterans when their minds are fixed on making their first or fiftieth champion.

In 1975 so many British exports are making the headlines. In Sweden the expected entry in classes is often more than treble what it would have been ten years ago. Stock from Birkfell, Lasara, Quakertown and other kennels is doing well. In New Zealand Lasara Landlubber gained ten C.C.s in eight months including two reserve best-in-shows. In the U.S.A. Ch. Ardenrun 'andsome of Purston, bred by Mr C. Oakley and exported by Mr M. Collings, excelled himself by winning the Terrier Group at the Westminster. In Spain Int. Ch. Kirkgordon Mariniello, bred and exported by Mrs M. Dickinson, has competed in Portgual, France and Spain with outstanding success. The list is almost endless but we all share in the satisfaction of knowing that British bred dogs lead the world.

Thomas Fall

Ch. Freshney Fiametta, 1947

B. Thurse

Ch. Barrister of Branston, 1950

Ch. Eoghan of Kendrum, 1954

Ch. Bandsman of Branston, 1960

2

The Breed Standard

IN Great Britain there are three Specialist Clubs, the senior one, of course, being The West Highland White Terrier Club, based in Scotland and known to one and all as The Scottish Club, founded in 1906. Shortly afterwards, in the same year, The West Highland White Terrier Club of England was formed. It was not until 1959 that a breed club started in Northern Ireland.

The standard we know today has altered very little from the time it was first set out and recognised by the Kennel Club, in about 1908. The interpretation in some instances is perhaps a little different, as for instance colour, which was always described as white, but rarely, as far as can be gathered, meant the same as we mean by white today. In all the old records I have come across it was freely admitted that a sandy or yellowish streak down the back was usually present and permitted. Now the description means what it says, and a poor-coloured coat is penalised.

The most significant change was made in 1948, at a joint meeting of the committees of the Scottish and English Clubs held in Edinburgh, when it was agreed that the height should be about eleven inches at the shoulder as against the previous eight to twelve inches which had been the accepted height from the days of the original standard. Also, the weight standard of 14 lb to 18 lb for dogs and 12 lb to 16 lb for bitches was abandoned and no weights, therefore, are shown in the present standard. In my opinion this was a grave error because now, except for height, there is no guide to body size and bone formation. A dog can be the correct height as laid down by the standard but be very light and shelly, and conversely, it could

C

be very coarse, due to having an over-heavy body. On the other hand, there must be enough body and bone to give the breed strength to fulfil its original purpose, which the dogs in the early days obviously had since they were regularly used for badger hunting. Of recent years there has been a tendency with some breeders to produce a West Highland White that looks, in body, like a Scottish Terrier. This is quite incorrect and should be guarded against.

The following is the Kennel Club Standard, reproduced by permission.

General Appearance. The General Appearance of the West Highland White Terrier is that of a small, game, hardy-looking terrier, possessed with no small amount of self-esteem, with a varminty appearance, strongly built, deep in chest and back ribs, level back and powerful quarters on muscular legs, and exhibiting in a marked degree a great combination of strength and activity. Movement should be free, straight and easy all round. In the front, the legs should be freely extended forward by the shoulder. The hind movement should be free, strong and close in under the body, so that when moving off the foot the body is pushed forward with some force. Stiff stilted movement behind is very objectionable.

Head and Skull. The skull should be slightly domed and when gripped across the forehead should present a smooth contour. There should be only a very slight tapering from the skull at the level of the ears to the eyes. The distance from the occiput to the eyes should be slightly greater than the length of the foreface. The head should be thickly coated with hair and carried at a right angle or less to the axis of the neck. On no account should the head be carried in the extended position. The foreface should gradually taper from the eye to the muzzle. There should be a distinct stop formed by heavy bone ridges, immediately above and slightly overhanging the eye, and a slight indentation between the eyes. The foreface should not dish or fall away quickly below the eyes where it should be well made up. The jaws should be strong and level. The nose must be black, should be fairly large, and forming a smooth contour with the rest of the muzzle. The nose must not project forward giving rise to a snipy appearance.

Eyes. Should be widely set apart, medium in size, as dark as possible in colour, slightly sunk in head, sharp and intelligent, which looking from under the heavy eyebrows imparts a piercing look. Full or light coloured eyes are objectionable.

Ears. Small, erect, and carried firmly, terminating in a sharp point. The hair of them should be short, smooth (velvety) and they should not be cut. The ears should be free from any fringe at the top. Round pointed, broad, large and thick ears are very objectionable, also ears too heavily coated with hair.

Mouth. Should be as broad between the canine teeth as is consistent with the sharp varminty expression demanded. The teeth should be large for the size of the dog, and should articulate in the following manner: the lower canines should lock in front of the upper canines. There should be six teeth between the canines of the upper and lower incisors. The upper incisors should slightly overlap the lower incisors, the inner aspect of the upper incisors being in contact with the outer aspect of the incisors. There should be no appreciable space between the incisors when the mouth is closed, ensuring a keen bite; a dead level mouth is not a fault.

Neck. The neck should be sufficiently long to allow the proper set on of head required, muscular and gradually thickening towards the base, allowing the neck to merge into nicely sloping shoulders, thus giving freedom of movement.

Forequarters. The shoulders should be sloped backwards. The shoulder blades should be broad and lie close to the chest wall. The joint formed by the shoulder blade and upper arm should be placed forward, on account of the obliquity of the shoulder blade, bringing the elbows well in, and allowing the foreleg to move freely, parallel to the axis of the body, like the pendulum of a clock. Forelegs should be short and muscular, straight and thickly covered with short hard hair.

Body. Compact. Level back, loins broad and strong. The chest should be deep and the ribs well arched in the upper half, presenting a flattish side appearance. The back ribs should be of considerable depth and the distance from the last rib of the quarters as short as is compatible with free movement of the body.

Hindquarters. Strong, muscular and wide across the top. Legs should be short and muscular and sinewy. The thighs very muscular and not too wide apart. The hocks gent and well set in under the body so as to be fairly close to each other when standing, walking or trotting. Cow hocks detract from the general appearance. Straight or weak hocks—both kinds are undesirable and should be guarded against.

Feet. The forefeet are larger than the hind ones, are round, proportionate in size, strong, thickly padded and covered with short hard hair. The hind feet are smaller and thickly padded. The under surface of the pads of feet and all nails should be preferably black.

Tail. 5 to 6 inches long, covered with hard hair, no feathers, as straight as possible, carried jauntily, not gay or carried over the back. A long tail is objectionable and on no account should tails be docked.

Coat. Colour pure white, must be double coated. The outer coat consists of hard hair, about 2 inches long, free from any curl. The under-coat which resembles fur, is short, soft and close. Open coats are objectionable.

Colour. Pure white.

Size. Size about 11 inches at the withers.

With a standard so briefly but clearly written it should be easy to form a mental picture, even to one who is not very familiar with the breed. Truly to appreciate the many sterling qualities and wonderful temperament of this fascinating terrier one must really own one or, if possible, two or more. One thing the standard fails to lay enough emphasis on is the character and adaptability and all-round purpose of this versatile dog, the best-tempered of all terrier breeds, who is a worker, game and energetic and yet able to adapt with ease to the artificial life of the city dweller. So distinctive is his white coat and black nose and piercing expression that he will always stand out in a crowd, and rarely passes along a street without drawing looks of admiration.

For anyone intending to breed West Highlands, whether for the occasional litter for pleasure or for more serious breeding, with sights set on the summit of success, which means at least one champion or more, then the standard must be studied until it is known by heart; not just casually but until it is known so well that any particular point leaps to mind. It may be difficult to breed the perfect Westie, but one should know instinctively what one is trying to achieve. To have some vague idea of what the standard is all about is not enough. It costs no more to rear a prospective champion than some ill-begotten pup with every imaginable fault, and there is a great deal more pleasure in looking at the result. First, let it be remembered that the West Highland is a working terrier. Not 'was' but 'is', and a true one is as tough as the rocks of its native land. It is a distinctive name —West Highland White Terrier—so descriptive that its name indicates what to expect from the breed: a dog that is hardy, tough and game, intelligent, cheerful and independent, and ready to do a good day's work. It must always be remembered that from their very earliest days they were highly thought of, chiefly for their ability to kill rats, hunt and kill badger, and to dig and squeeze their way into almost inaccessible places. It is important, therefore, to know what sort of ribs they should have and why so small a dog has such muscle and strength and all else that makes up a really typical specimen of the breed. Unfortunately, today many never get the opportunity to show their skill as vermin killers, but to be true to the breed their structure must be right so that if occasion ever arises they may be a credit to their ancestors.

One of the most descriptive phrases in the standard is in the paragraph under the heading General Appearance—'A small, game, hardy terrier, possessed with no small amount of self esteem', a description that is exactly right and describes the whole dog in a nutshell. Add to this the piercing look in their eyes, the pricked attentive ears, the proud way the head is held, the look of quiet assurance and self confidence, the free gay movement that makes one think of a bonny Scotsman with his kilt swinging to the sound of the pipes, the gay devil-may-care look, the smart appearance with a straight white coat and black points, and a substantial though not too heavy body, and the whole portrait is of a dog with great vitality and strength in a neat compact frame.

Although no mention of weight is made in the standard of today, it is generally accepted that the ideal for a dog is about 16 to 18 lb, though some almost certainly weigh considerably more. It should be carefully watched to see that they do not become too big or coarse, nor, on the other hand, should they be too small. A bitch should be proportionately smaller, with a weight of about 14 to 16 lb.

In his book, *The West Highland White Terrier*, written in 1911, Holland Buckley wrote that Brogach, the sire of Morven, was 17 lb weight, Atholl, Morven's best son, 16 lb, Model, the best great-grandson of Brogath, 16 lb.

They should have neither the appearance of the Scottish Terrier with its lower-slung heavy body nor the lightness of bone and body of the Cairn Terrier. For weight and size the West Highland is fairly and squarely between its two Scottish cousins. It will be a great pity if the lovely head we associate with the breed is ever allowed to be spoilt.

It must be remembered that the standard says, 'the distance from the occiput to the eyes should be slightly greater than the length of the foreface'. If this description is kept firmly in mind the long foreface, which occasionally creeps in, will rapidly disappear.

It is important, too, that the muzzle is not thin and nipped in. It is a strong foreface because it needs to have room in the jaw bone to contain those good strong teeth which have the power to kill, at one snap, a good-sized rat.

The possession of a decided 'stop' is vital if the head is to look right. The stop is formed by the heavy bone ridge or eyebrow, with a slight indentation between the eyes. Without a good stop the head is almost always long and lean in appearance, the eyes narrow-set, and the typical expression quite lost.

A good dark well-shapen eye of medium size is important. The socket is, near enough, almond-shaped, and together with the black eye rims and the very dark eye the expression gives a piercing look. Nothing spoils the expression more than a light

eye, which is quite out of keeping and should never be con-
doned because it spoils the characteristic charm of the true
West Highland.

Ears, too, are another feature vital to correct expression, and
in some ways they do more for the head than the eyes. The real
terrier look and character can be seen when the dog is on the
alert and the ears are pricked forward inquisitively, asking,
listening, and all-aquiver for any exciting bit of sport that may
be coming up next. Neat, well-pricked ears are most desirable,
placed so that they look neither too wide nor too narrow. They
must not be too wide at the base, too thick, or even a bit soft.
Carried alertly they are a great asset. Carried too wide gives the

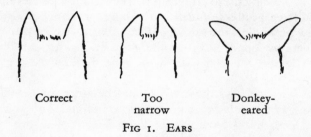

Correct   Too   Donkey-
           narrow   eared

FIG 1. EARS

expression a mulish and unhappy look not at all characteristic
of the breed.

The nose, which must be black, should protrude beyond the
end of the muzzle only very slightly and should blend into the
foreface. A large nose is unsightly. Occasionally the colour of
a nose will fade a little and become a pale brown, but this, if it
happens, is generally only in the winter months or, sometimes,
if a dog is not in top condition. It is usually only a passing
phase of a few weeks' duration. Years ago I had a dog with the
blackest of toe nails, but at the beginning of winter they
turned a very pale brown and stayed so until the spring, when
they again reverted to black. Oddly enough, his nose was
black all the time.

The description of the mouth, in the standard, seems a little inadequate since it makes no mention of the number of teeth in the mouth as a whole, and refers only to the six incisors in top and bottom jaws between the canines, and of the scissor fashion bite of the top incisors over the lower incisors. Molars and pre-molars are not considered so important in the United Kingdom as they are in some other countries, and they are not mentioned in the standard, which is a pity because in some circumstances they can be important. In at least one continental country dogs are not eligible for show, and in others heavily penalised by some judges, if their teeth do not conform to set standards, but more of this in another chapter. In a fully grown dog a full complement of teeth is forty-two, six incisors and two canines in each jaw. The molars and pre-molars can be remarkably difficult to count up correctly, but a perfect mouth should have a full set of teeth, although points are not lost here if a few pre-molars are missing. They, the pre-molars, are often quite late in coming through the gums and sometimes do not appear before the dog is eight or nine months old, or even more.

The standard says the teeth should be large for the size of the dog. It certainly gives great pleasure to find a good strong set of teeth but I have yet to find a Westie that, even with smaller than normal teeth or an elderly dog with some missing, could not kill a rat with the greatest of ease. The strength must, to a large degree, lie in the jaw, as I have personally known a four-months-old puppy catch and kill a rat, and the way they can gnaw through a marrow or shin bone is quite extraordinary.

The final item of charm to a lovely head is, of course, the hair, which is usually referred to as 'furnishing'. It grows naturally and needs no great amount of trimming. The hair on the head is a little softer than elsewhere on the body and usually needs only the ends tidied up to keep it from covering the eyes completely and hiding the expression.

The neck and forequarters are almost indivisible, in that one part depends so much on the other. The neck must be of good proportions, strong and muscular and fairly long, but not too long. A neck that is too long can make a dog look unbalanced and is almost as bad, though not quite, as one with too little neck. The neck must merge smoothly into the shoulders, which it will do if the shoulders have the correct lay-back. This is of the utmost importance.

The apex of the shoulder blades should be very close together, almost, but not quite, touching. The scapula makes almost a right angle with the humerus. If the shoulders have

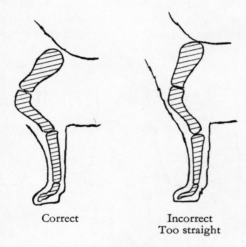

Correct   Incorrect
         Too straight

FIG. 2. SHOULDER PLACEMENT

the correct lay-back the back will be shorter and the neck longer. If the shoulders are straight the whole conformation is spoilt and the shoulders become like those of a cart-horse instead of a thorough-bred.

Together with good shoulder placement there will be the long free stride which really covers the ground and so delights the eye of the beholder. Hand in hand with straight shoulders will go a stilted gait, when the feet seem to be very busy getting nowhere.

When a well-made dog is moving away from you in a straight line it should be impossible to see past the hindquarters to the shoulders. If the dog is heavy and thick on the shoulders at the point where the scapula and humerus join, then the dog will have 'loaded' shoulders, which give an appearance of coarseness and heaviness.

The best description I ever heard of shoulders was made by Dr Russell of 'Cruben' fame. He said that good shoulders resembled more nearly the neck of a champagne bottle than that of a beer bottle.

The shoulders and front quarters should be refined in comparison to the hindquarters which have the muscular strength and roundness that can supply the power that gives the great

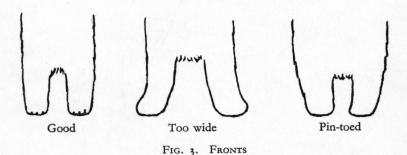

Good   Too wide   Pin-toed

FIG. 3. FRONTS

drive for the strong thrusting movement so typical of a West Highland.

The West Highland White should be fairly wide across the loin with a feeling of firmness and strength under an out-spanned hand. The stifles must be well bent but not exaggeratedly so. The hind legs must have really good muscle, for here lies all the driving power. Straight stifles and lean shanks go together with cow hocks and weak stilted movement, about the worst faults a West Highland can possess.

A good tail is a great asset. It must be short, thick at the root, gradually tapering to a point. Although the standard says the tail should be about six inches long, most people prefer it to be shorter, between four or five inches. A better guide is that the tail should be in proportion to the size of the dog. When a dog is standing alert, with head and tail well held up, the tip of the tail should be about level with the top of the head between the ears. It is most important that the tail has a good set, high rather than low, which quite detracts from the appearance. A well-shaped tail, inclining just the slightest bit, but no more, to-

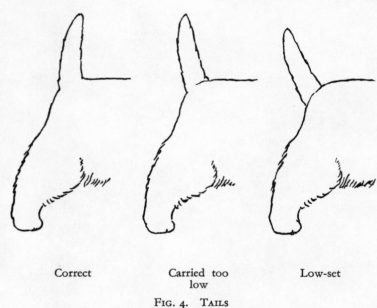

Correct   Carried too   Low-set
low

FIG. 4. TAILS

wards the ears, looks most natural and also gives the impression of a short back. Thin, long or gay tails are undesirable.

Good tight feet, well padded, are another essential. Thin feet, down on the pasterns with toes splayed out, do not fit in with the picture of a game hardy terrier that can do a hard day's work on rough ground. Last, but not least, is their weather-resistant jacket, a coat that is rain- and wind-proof, to give protection to its wearer as he fights his way through a bramble hedge after rabbit. The soft undercoat provides the warmth, and the top coat repels most of the rain. The genuine white adds the final touch of smartness; any other breed looks drab and ordinary standing beside a well-kept Westie.

It is small wonder that with so many good things wrapped up in so small a parcel, discerning owners who want a really distinctive dog around come back time and again for another West Highland to replace old faithfuls who have passed on to their happy hunting grounds.

3

Planning a Kennel

THE majority of kennels come into being as a result of a dog being bought as a family pet with no other purpose than to enjoy its companionship and love. Quite by chance, someone suggests it is worth showing, particulars are obtained of the next local show and, believe it or not, before the owner knows anything more she is coming home with a red card and the assurance from a friendly judge that 'you have a champion there'. Whether this proverbial beginner's luck lasts or not, more often than not freedom has been signed away, the disease of dog breeding and showing has been caught, and the dog owner must resign himself to a lifetime of ecstasy and despair. The real dog lover rarely gives up. If he has had a bad day, there is always next time. Before long the original pet is supplemented with one or two bitches, which is all right in a small house with a small breed like the Westie, but when they have puppies even the most strong-minded find excuses for keeping a puppy from this or that litter. That is when the trouble starts, for unless outside kennels are erected there is not much room left in the house for the owner.

Kennels today are designed for every size and shape of dog; most are good but many are too small and dark and uncomfortable, especially for the long, dark, dreary days of winter.

First consideration, of course, is a suitable site and space for the chosen kennel and run. The ground must be well drained and the kennel should, if possible, face south with room to have pens or runs on either side.

Profiting from my early experience with the first kennel I ever bought, I advise against anything that cannot be walked into and stood upright in while working. There is no joy on a wet winter's day in feeding puppies with one's head in the kennel and the rear end out in the wet and cold.

Plan to build the kennel or kennels as near as possible to the house, for our breed likes human companionship and does not thrive when shut away. They are inquisitive little creatures and like to know what is going on. A largish building will cost more but will be worth the extra expense in the comfort acquired, when spending hours giving its inmates the attention they need.

As there are many restrictions in these days, it is best to find out from the local council if planning permission is necessary and it will be if the house is in a residential area. Also, if you have close neighbours, find out their attitude to your project, otherwise they may not be co-operative and will complain about barking, and so on. Time and money will be wasted if, after erecting smart new kennels, near neighbours complain to the council that the dogs disturb them.

Usually, the intention is to limit the numbers kept to at the most three or four bitches but when, having bred two or more litters, the temptation to keep the best puppy from each litter has proved irresistible, numbers soon outstrip the original plan. While about it, therefore, it is better to allow for expansion. Before beginning to build, try to get some good, workable ideas from other established kennels. They have probably thought of things that could be improved in their own buildings and will freely advise against the mistakes they feel they made when they were drawing up plans for their kennels originally.

A good deal of thought needs to be given to eventual requirements before any building is erected. If the plan is to limit the number of dogs kept at any one time to six, with probably one or two of them living in the house at times, a building of about 20 to 24 ft long by 10 to 12 ft wide should be sufficient. This could easily be divided into three compartments, with reasonable space for dogs and their attendant to move around. Always guard against overcrowding or cramped quarters. There are many good designs of sectional building, and I have even seen a sectional garage erected and then divided up to suit individual requirements, but it was then necessary to put in additional windows.

With wooden kennels it is essential to insulate all external walls with hardboard, packing the space between the outer wall and the hardboard with wood wool or, better, lining it with polystrynol. It is inadvisable to use glass fibre as an in-filler as this could prove dangerous should a dog decide to try to chew through the wall. Although unlikely, it could happen.

When dividing up the kennel it is as well to plan for a corridor of adequate width the whole length of the building, to give easy access to each compartment. If possible, a small section should be left as a working area for grooming etc., with cupboard and shelves for storage of tools, toilet requisites and first-aid kit.

The divisions between each compartment should be at least 4 ft 6 inches high and constructed of chain-link fencing, of heavy gauge, on timber framing. Should it be required to segregate a compartment completely, solid portable wooden panels could be fitted within the timber frame of the chain-link partitions.

Lighting and heating must also be available in the kennel, and the safest and most satisfactory way is to use electricity, the installation of which should be carried out by a qualified electrician. No electrical fitting should be within reach of a dog.

Should it be thought desirable to heat the kennel during the winter months two infra-red 750-watt strip-heaters, thermostatically controlled, should be adequate. Most kennels need some form of heat, and dogs are more contented when the air is slightly warm. If it is proposed to use the kennel for whelping or puppy rearing, points should be provided for 250-watt infra-red dull emitters to hang directly over the whelping box. I have found the Elstein agricultural infra-red radiators most effective, resulting in contented mothers and babies. For puppies to thrive they must be comfortably warm. Some heat, therefore, is almost always required for the first week or two, and through the winter it will be required for an indefinite period. The height of the lamp above the box should be carefully adjusted and the instructions supplied with each heater strictly adhered to. These heaters can be obtained from most dog equipment specialists at Championship Shows or from P. & R. Electrical (London) Ltd, Pearl House, Acton, London, W.3.

Sleeping boxes should always be raised off the floor to avoid draughts. Dogs always seem to prefer to have a box to go into rather than an open bench on which to sleep. The most commonly used is probably the ordinary tea chest, adapted so easily for a small dog, and quite draught-proof. To lift the box off the floor it is quite simple to fix a length of 1 in by 1½ in timber on each side of the bottom of the chest. A piece of timber about 6 inches high fixed along the bottom front will keep the bedding in place. More elaborate arrangements for sleeping can be made if required, and ready-made cages may be bought with half-barred fronts and doors so that the dogs may be kept enclosed at night. This arrangement is quite good as long as the dogs are not shut in for too long, nor confining the dogs during the day time. I do not approve of dogs having to spend a large part of each and every day in a cage. No doubt it is possible to keep a far larger number at one time under those conditions, but no self-respecting West Highland should have to endure it.

Let the kennels be as near to the house as convenient because they need the companionship of humans as much as possible. If the dogs can have a good view of comings and goings they are going to be very much happier. They really do like to know what is going on.

The outside runs or pens should be formed with 4 ft-high chain-link fencing on concrete posts, if possible, but good timber or steel will suffice. The bottom line wire should be fixed as close to the ground as possible and secured to the stakes driven into the ground at intervals. This is important as West Highlands are expert excavators and will leave no stone unturned and no sod 'un-dug' if given half a chance.

The pens should be divided as required and a gate of adequate size should be provided to give access to each pen. The pens should be as long as possible to give plenty of scope for the dogs to chase about and amuse themselves. Long pens

Thomas Fall

Ch. Calluna the Poacher, aged 10½ years

Capt Bower judges Ch. Wolvey Play Girl, shown by Mrs Pacey,
and Ch. Bandsman of Branston, shown by the author.

Ch. Waideshouse Woodpecker, 1963

Ch. Petriburg Mark of Polteana, 1963

are better than square ones as they can extend themselves more when racing other dogs in adjacent pens. In reason this type of exercise is very beneficial for warming up and for developing good, well-muscled quarters, so important in this breed. Grass pens are pleasant in summer but of little use in winter when they soon become like ploughed fields. The best way to have both surfaces is to grass the centre of each pen and to provide a wide strip of concrete or paving stones all the way along the sides. All pens should be provided with raised benches on which the dogs can rest off the damp ground.

If the pen is large enough, a suitable shrub planted in the middle adds greatly to their enjoyment. Puppies especially get much pleasure and can have great fun and games dashing underneath the outspread branches and romping round and about it. Straight concrete pens look oh so neat and tidy but are too terribly dreary for lively little characters like West Highlands.

If, after a time, it is decided to expand, and more kennelling is needed, it will have to be decided whether to build a separate puppy house or a very secure kennel for bitches on heat. Everyone has their own ideas about first priorities, which vary according to the type of business it is intended to conduct. Always study the comfort and well-being of the dogs first, and never keep more than can be properly cared for.

If there are good outbuildings that can be converted into kennels, so much the better. Brick-built stables and barns, when lined and made draught-proof, give so much more room than sectionalised timber kennels and there is almost un-limited space for exercise under cover in inclement weather. It can be a slow job adapting these buildings to suit one's particular needs, but when eventually accomplished they can be a real joy to the dogs, owner and attendants. A large barn can be converted to house a great number of dogs in comfort. In the worst of winters, with weeks of snow and outside exercise impossible, the dogs can be kept busy and interested. Once the building has been satisfactorily lined throughout and divided up as required the living conditions are ideal for all times of the year, cool in summer and warm in winter.

D

If using this type of building be sure to let in plenty of extra windows wherever possible. Dark dreary kennels should never be tolerated.

If a fairly large number of dogs are to be kept it will soon be found most desirable to have a kennel kitchen for preparing the dogs' food and where the feeding dishes can be washed, stacked and put ready for the next mealtime. If hot and cold water is available dirty dishes are quickly disposed of after every meal. An electric mincer does away with the tedious job of mincing pounds of meat by hand. The more efficiently every-day chores are planned the greater amount of time there is to spend with the dogs. A separate place for isolating a sick or injured dog is a great asset; it should be heated and quiet.

No matter how good the kennels are every dog enjoys being taken up to the house for a change and treated as a house pet. Two or three can often be brought into the house to sleep and then returned to the kennels in the morning, while others can come to the house during the day and return to sleep in the kennel. This sort of custom is much more important than is often realised. To some it may seem an unnecessary bit of extra work but it is the sort of thing that pays high dividends in building an equable-tempered dog, who is not nervous and who responds to all with whom it comes in contact, quietly confident that the world is a very nice place for little dogs. These are the dogs that make the most of themselves in the show ring. They are so interested in all that is going on around them that they enjoy life and show it by their happy alertness.

4

Breeding

To make a success of breeding the first essential is to start with a good bitch, for the old saying that, 'The strength of a kennel lies in its bitches' is as true now as it always was. It is not disputed that the stud dog plays a very important part but in founding a kennel the first priority must go to quality bitches.

A great deal of thought is needed, first in choosing the bitch, and then in finding the most suitable mate with blood lines in common. The more that is known of the bitch and her ancestors the better. To know that her sire and dam consistently produce a certain desirable type is reassuring and will prove a help in deciding what pattern to follow in breeding plans. Assess the bitch carefully both as to good and weak points, not forgetting the importance of temperament.

Should you wish, and who does not, to establish a strain easily recognisable as particularly your own, you may be sure that it is going to take many years of dedicated work and attention to detail. Endeavour to stick always to the type that is your ideal.

If you are a beginner don't think that anything will do to start with. Choose a bitch from a line that is renowned for its ability to produce with almost monotonous regularity a succession of good ones of both sexes.

Price too often being the governing factor a newcomer will often decide to make do with something a little inferior at less cost, hoping that the use of a good champion dog will be sufficient to counterbalance any faults and failings the bitch may have. Just occasionally such a mating may by a lucky fluke produce a good one, even perhaps a champion, but it is rather unlikely. Years of disappointment and frustration can follow this type of 'flash in the pan' success simply because there is no real quality background. The beginner will wonder why it seems impossible to repeat the original success, and put it down to bad luck. Luck? Of course there is an element of luck sometimes, and one should be duly grateful for it, but more often it is good judgement and common sense, and the fact that the right foundation stock was used in the beginning, having first made an extensive study of blood lines and followed out a well-considered breeding schedule.

There are many good kennels who, over the years, have worked out for themselves a sound breeding policy. If a bitch has been obtained from one of these successful kennels with an established line of breeding, then you will be wise to ask and be ready to accept the sound advice that will be readily given if asked for. You may be treated to a learned discourse on the theory of Mendel, if your mentor is blessed with scientific and biological knowledge, but it is more likely that you will be dealing with a breeder who is concerned more with the practical knowledge gained through years of hard and sometimes bitter experience. The experienced breeder will have strong feelings about line breeding, inbreeding and blood lines and can usually produce a good collection of pedigrees going back several generations to prove a point.

With a quality bitch that satisfies you in all the essentials, breeding back to her grand-sire or to a half-brother is considered a good plan. However, if neither of these is available, look around for some other with suitable blood lines as near as possible to the desired type and possessing a pedigree that contains at least three or more of the most dominant dogs recurring in your bitch's pedigree. The experienced breeder when studying a pedigree is able to conjure up a picture of the dog concerned, seeing not only a collection of names but conformation, character and temperament.

Do not let the bogy of the word 'inbreeding', about which so much nonsense is talked, frighten you. The term inbreeding is applied when mother and son or father and daughter or brother and sister are bred together. Inbreeding is not common in West Highlands but at times it has been used with satisfactory results. It is one way of stamping the type, but it is vital that both should be absolutely sound and as near perfection as any dog can be. The temperament must be quite reliable, with no sign of nervousness. It would be folly indeed to inbreed with something unsound either mentally or physically, for faults as well as virtues are intensified by inbreeding. Only the best should be kept, and if any dog or bitch shows the slightest weakness or fault he or she should not be kept, or bred from. The beginner should seek advice from a reliable source before embarking on any plan to inbreed. At the right time it can be good, and helps to fix a desired type, but you must know what you are about and it should not be lightly undertaken.

Line breeding, which is generally considered to be good, is to mate grandfather to grand-daughter or half-brothers and sisters. Unless, of course, both dog and bitch are good specimens of the breed, line breeding is unlikely to achieve anything of quality.

To outcross is to breed to another line that is completely unrelated. This is generally resorted to only after several generations of line-breeding and its object is to bring in fresh blood; for example, in the hope of regaining size if it is considered that the progeny are getting too small.

It should be possible to learn quite a lot from the first one or two litters you breed. Get someone, either the owner of the stud dog or the breeder of the bitch, to look at the puppies and advise you which, if any, to keep. If you do sell them all and are able to keep in touch with them in their new homes, so much the better. By the time you are ready to breed from the bitch a second time you will be able to decide to repeat the mating or try another dog. If the first litter produces nothing of outstanding quality then see if another sire can do better. Much has been written, by a famous breeder of another breed, against repeat matings, suggesting that each succeeding litter is less satisfactory than the last. I cannot accept this as from my own experience I have proved it to be quite contrary to the facts. If it is found that a certain dog suits a bitch and can produce champions in successive litters there is surely nothing to be gained by trying elsewhere. Whenever I was ill-advised enough to try another dog the results were always very disappointing. Bloom of Branston bred to Ch. Hookwood Mentor three times and produced a champion in each litter. Binty of Branston mated to Ch. Barrister of Branston also was responsible for another three champions. Binty also had one other champion when mated to Barrister's full brother Ch. Brisk of Branston. Bono of Branston likewise produced three champions when mated to Ch. Banker of Branston on three consecutive occasions. Ch. Brindie of Branston also bred a champion on each of the three occasions that she was mated to Ch. Sollershott Sun-up, but with Brindie, alas, wanting very much to bring in another line, I sent her on a visit to another very good dog twice, but with disappointing results.

There must be many other kennels with similar successful repeat matings. One that particularly comes to mind are Miss F. Cook's 'Famechecks'. In four litters Ch. Famecheck Lucky Mascot when mated to her nephew Ch. Famecheck Gay Crusader produced five champions. Surely that is successful breeding by any standard. Again, out of Ch. Famecheck Lucky Charm, bred to her cousin Ch. Happy Knight, came three champions out of two litters. Unfortunately Happy Knight died very young or there would probably have been even more champions.

The Stud Dog

A stud dog should look masculine. He should have all the traits one associates with the male. A good strong head carried proudly and with a determined, assertive look. That does not mean that he is a born fighter but rather that he will stand his ground and dare anyone to touch what is his. He must always be kept in the prime of condition. Well fed on good meat, both raw and cooked. An egg each day if he enjoys them, also milk. Biscuit should be only a secondary item of his diet as he should not be allowed to become unduly fat. With mainly meat he will be hard and active. A good stud dog is worth his keep and should not be kept short of anything to keep him in the peak of condition.

If a bitch is to be mated during the day he should have his

early morning exercise and then be kept quiet until the mating is accomplished. Always insist that any bitch that is visiting him arrives well before feeding time. Never allow a dog to be used directly he has had a meal.

It is wise to limit the number of bitches that may visit him especially while he is still young. The age a dog should first be at stud varies according to the way he has matured. A West Highland is usually ready to serve a bitch at ten or eleven months but after that he should not be used more than once a month until he is considerably older. Later, a strong healthy dog will manage one or more in a week. Mrs Pacey, who was such a great authority on everything pertaining to dogs, told me that she had found that if a dog was used too frequently when he was young he would go off stud work for a time.

With a young dog giving his first service it is better if the bitch has been bred from previously. If he is started with a maiden bitch, who may be a little difficult or refuse completely to be mated, it can be most unfortunate and sap his confidence.

If much stud work is to be undertaken it is best to have a small room or kennel kept solely for the purpose. All that is necessary is that it should be clean and uncluttered. When scrubbed out it is better to use strong soda-water rather than a strong-smelling disinfectant which can sometimes put a dog off, the scent from the bitch being camouflaged. The only 'furniture' required is a cage or travelling box, in which the bitch can be placed after mating or any other time, a table, a bowl of cold water, cotton-wool, a towel and a jar of Vaseline.

Be sure that the door of the room you are using is securely closed. Nothing could be worse than to allow a bitch in season to escape. If the bitch is good-tempered and ready for mating she will like to flirt and play for a few minutes and it is quite delightful to watch this preliminary lovemaking. As soon as the bitch seems ready to stand and turns her tail invitingly sideways, hold her steadily so that the dog may position himself comfortable. A little Vaseline smeared on the finger and then inserted into the vaginal passage will usually facilitate an easier mating. Some people prefer the mating to take place on a table, and it certainly saves backache, but not all dogs like this procedure. If, however, you do use a table, be sure it is firm and substantial and covered with thick material such as sacking so that the animals can get a firm foothold. Never allow your attention to be distracted while they are on the table, particularly during the actual mating or when they are 'tied'; a slip off the end of the table might cause serious injury to one or both. Once the mating has been successfully accomplished put the bitch in the box to rest for half an hour or so. If the bitch objects to the dog very strongly directly she sets eyes on him, however, more likely than not she is either not ready or that her season is over. Owners are not always too sure of the day their bitches come into season, and in any case the length of time each individual bitch is actually on heat varies quite a lot. Some are quite ready at ten days or earlier, others at fourteen to sixteen days, or even longer, *but the eleventh day is about normal*. An experienced stud dog will, however, rarely show much interest unless the bitch is quite ready.

If it is possible to have an assistant to hold the bitch, so much the better, for it allows the other person to give the necessary attention to the dog. The dog can be helped quite considerably by placing one hand under the bitch and slightly raising the vulva. If there is no stricture or obstruction and the bitch stands quietly the dog should penetrate without trouble. If, on the other hand, after repeated attempts he is unable to mate the bitch, it is better to make a further examination of her before the dog exhausts himself. Dip the finger into Vaseline, gently insert the finger into the vagina, and if there is a stricture it will be quickly found. If slight, it can be easily broken with the finger and there should be no more difficulty. If the bitch is malformed or has some more serious obstruction, however, it will be necessary for a veterinary surgeon to examine her more thoroughly.

Directly the dog's penis penetrates and the dog is obviously working, hold him firmly in position until such time as the tie is complete. When the dog and bitch are satisfactorily tied the dog is usually ready to turn and will lift one hind leg over the bitch's back so that they will be standing tail to tail. Most people consider it more satisfactory if there is a tie, but some dogs never attain it, and yet beget good litters. Always talk quietly to them both while they are in this position, and see that the bitch remains steady. If she is allowed to fidget the dog may be injured. It is best to hold one of the dog's and one of the bitch's hind legs together so that it is impossible for them to move before the penis is withdrawn. Directly the mating is completed place the bitch in a cage or box so that she may rest quietly for half an hour or so. Make sure that the dog is fully retracted before returning him to his normal kennel or living quarters.

If the mating has been satisfactory there seems little value in repeating the performance, but sometimes the owner of the bitch will request that two matings be given. Most owners of a stud will accede to the request if feasible, but if the dog is in great demand it may not always be possible to do so. If a second mating is given, it may be either the next day or the next but one. If a maiden bitch has been reluctant to be mated then it is desirable that she has a second service, when she will probably be more co-operative.

It is the usual practice to give a free service on the next heat if the bitch proves not to be in whelp after the first, but it should be made quite clear that if there are no puppies the owner of the stud dog should be informed without delay.

Stud fees should always be paid at the time of service and, in return, the pedigree of the dog used should be given to the owner of the bitch.

5

Whelping

THE period of gestation is sixty-three days so there is plenty of time to make preparation for the expected litter.

When the bitch has finished her season let her return to her normal routine without any fuss. It is usually about five weeks before it is possible to say with any certainty that puppies are on the way. Until such time, let her have the ordinary exercise to which she has been accustomed, but discourage attempts at jumping on or off boxes or rushing up and down steps. Don't be too anxious to find out, before it becomes obvious, whether she is in whelp or not. Harm can be done by palpating a bitch to feel if she has puppies. Try to curb your natural impatience; at five weeks, or a day or two more, it will probably be evident without any doubt that she is to have a family.

Now is the time to give her any extras you have decided will be beneficial. Guard against the temptation to overfeed, and so make her too fat. If she has been used to one large meal in the evening it will be best to give an extra feed of meat, either raw or lightly cooked, whichever suits her best, in the middle of the day, at the same time reducing the starchy parts of the evening meal. At this stage she should be having calcium-lactate, either in tablet or powder form. If she regularly clears up all her food it is easier to put the calcium on the evening meal; it is quite tasteless. If she is a bit dainty, however, and tends to leave some on her dish, the tablet form is more satisfactory since one can then be sure that the necessary quantity has been consumed. Recently I have found that the regular use of seaweed powder is very beneficial to all my dogs, at all ages, and my breeding bitches continue to have it all the time they are in whelp. A generous half-teaspoonful on their food seems to be taken with relish, and it is a very simple way of giving a balanced mineral and vitamin supplement. If the bitch enjoys a basin of milk and raw egg in the last weeks of pregnancy, so much the better. It is the quality of the food rather than the quantity that counts at this stage.

During the last month give one 3-grain raspberry-leaf tablet every day, and in the last ten days one teaspoonful of linseed oil B.P. These last two are recognised by most people to be very helpful towards easy whelpings. By the time the bitch is into the seventh week she will usually take things more quietly of her own accord. If she is free to exercise or rest as and when she wishes she will not overtire herself or do more than she feels able to do. I never like to see a bitch exercised on a lead at this time; the freedom of a garden, even if a fairly small one, is far better.

Many bitches whelp anything from two to four days early and it should therefore be seen that all preparations are made in good time. If there is a regular whelping kennel kept solely for that purpose, all will be ready to hand and the bitch can be accustomed to sleeping there for the last ten days or so of pregnancy. They show that they know what it is all about, for they look pleased and contented to have a place to themselves where they can rest in peace and quiet. Many people, however, whenever possible like to have the bitch close at hand in a quiet room in the house when the actual time arrives. It is certainly a great convenience if it is to be an all-night affair, as it so often is. Trailing backwards and forwards to the kennel on a long, cold winter's night is no joy to anyone, as I know from experience. At all events wherever it is decided that the puppies shall be born, in the house or in the kennel, the important thing is that all is ready and waiting and the bitch feeling quite at home and satisfied with the arrangements you have made for her.

Let the whelping place be clear of anything that is not absolutely essential. Necessities are: as many layers of paper on the floor as you can possibly manage, the whelping box, and a bench or small firm table on which to lay the necessary equipment. You will also require a large roll of cotton-wool, any clean pieces of cotton sheeting available, towels, Dettol, a basin of water, and scissors. During the whelping the room temperature should be kept around 65° to 70° Fahrenheit. An infra-red lamp hung over the whelping box at a suitable height will keep the bed warm and dry. It is best to have the lamp hung by a chain so that the height can be adjusted to give more or less heat. Even during a warm night newly born puppies easily get chilled, and the more quickly they are dried and warm the less risks there are of losses.

The first signs that a bitch is nearing her time is often when she refuses a meal, sometimes about twelve hours or more before the actual whelping starts. She will probably become very restless and tear up the bedding in the whelping box, and for that, if no other reason, it is just as well that the whelping box is thickly lined with several layers of clean newspapers covered with a small soft piece of old blanket. A good supply of pieces of blanket are invaluable.

Everyone has their own ideas on whelping boxes and many good types can be obtained from different manufacturers, but my preference is for a strongly constructed, tongued and grooved wooden box on a substantial frame. The box should be plenty long enough for the bitch to lie full length in comfort. The most suitable size I have found is 2 ft 6 in × 2 ft wide and 18 in high. It has a hinged lid on top, which can be raised when the infra-red lamp is in use, and closed to keep out draughts when the lamp is not being used. It also has a hinged front that can be let down to give the bitch easy access during the time she is whelping and, later, raised and secured by two thumb-screws to prevent the puppies from falling out of the bed.

Once it is evident that labour has genuinely started it is best to be close at hand all the time. Most bitches seem to derive quite a lot of comfort from the presence of their owner. The bitch usually pants very quickly and becomes very restless, getting in and out of the box, tearing up the bedding and then pacing back and forth, usually with the tail tucked underneath the body. The length of time taken for a bitch to produce her first puppy varies a good deal. Some will produce a puppy only half an hour or so after the onset of straining, while others may take perhaps two hours or more. Some whelp so easily that one is hardly aware that a puppy has arrived, but others make much more ado about it and will cry out in pain continuously. If when the puppy is partly born it seems to get stuck and the bitch is unable to expel it completely, then it is time to give assistance. Using either a piece of cotton-wool or cotton sheeting, as the bitch strains grasp the part of the puppy that has appeared and pull slowly but firmly until it is safely delivered. Puppies are normally born head first but occasionally they arrive feet first. This is known as a breech birth and, more often than not, the cause of a difficult birth. It is useless to be squeamish at such a time, nor give way to agitation. If the bitch is given assistance every time she strains, in a minute or so it will be over. If the bitch has had a struggle with the first puppy she will be only too glad to let someone get on with the process of cleaning it up for her. If the bag in which it is born has not ruptured, then break it quickly with your fingers and, holding the puppy in your left hand, let the bag and afterbirth hang downwards so that the umbilical cord can be cut with a sharp pair of sterilised scissors. It is better to leave the umbilical cord too long rather than cut it too short; about an inch and a half is safe enough. This quickly dries up and in a couple of days will fall away, the bitch meanwhile giving it plenty of washing with her tongue. Dry the puppy as quickly as possible in a warm soft towel and when it is beginning to move strongly give it to the proud mother.

If all goes well, after a short rest she will start to strain again and repeat the whole performance, but usually once the first puppy is born the rest follow without too much trouble. Sometimes after one or two puppies she will take a longer rest, but there is no hard and fast rule, and one can only wait patiently. It is always as well to have a strong cardboard box ready with a rubber hot-water bottle and soft pieces of blanket and cotton-wool in case the whelping is long drawn out. If it is the puppies can be placed in this box while the bitch is concerning herself with producing another puppy. If the puppies are left in the bed and the bitch is experiencing much trouble she may trample on them, make them uncomfortable, and they will cry incessantly. It is better to pop them into a warm box for a while to sleep contentedly. With luck, an easy whelping may well be all over in three or four hours or even less. Some people prefer to let the bitch be entirely responsible for cleaning up of the puppies, and let her bite the cord and eat up the afterbirth. It used to be generally believed that there was some value to the bitch in this, but in my experience the bitch, although she will eat the afterbirth, will often vomit it up again in a very short time, making a very unpleasant mess in the bed. I believe it is better to remove each afterbirth oneself, and should one become detached from the puppy and not arrive when the puppy is born, as sometimes happens, it is necessary to keep a sharp eye on the bitch in case of a serious rise in temperature, for if an afterbirth is left behind it will almost certainly cause trouble unless prompt steps are taken to avoid complications.

If the whelping has been straightforward and the services of the veterinary surgeon have not been required it is still as well to let him examine the mother next day and, if he considers it necessary, give an antibiotic injection to counteract possible infection. A few people still believe in leaving everything to nature, but there are times when taking advantage of modern medicine saves a lot of worry and, more important by far, saves your bitch a lot of unnecessary suffering.

If by some misfortune the whelping does not go according to plan do not hesitate to call a veterinary surgeon in good time so that he can take whatever steps seem necessary, even a Caesarian operation if required.

If at the beginning of her labour the bitch after three hours of straining does not seem to be making any headway then do get professional help. Any good veterinary surgeon would rather make an unnecessary visit than be called out to a case that is past all help. If he should decide that a Caesarian is necessary, it is better undertaken before the bitch becomes overtired and weakened with fruitless straining. Twenty years or more ago few puppies used to survive a Caesarian operation but now it is an exception to lose any puppies if the operation is done in good time. In a very short time, three or four hours, the bitch will be back home and in her bed with a healthy litter of puppies contentedly feeding. After that, apart from a little stiffness she will quickly be back to normal.

Once all the puppies have arrived, unless the bed is in a great deal of mess, it is best to leave changing the bedding until she is rested. Before leaving her to rest give her a basin of warm milk, as much as a pint, to which a dessertspoonful of glucose powder has been added, and some honey or sugar. It will be necessary to hold this so that she can drink it comfortably without disturbing herself too much. After that you can safely take a well-earned rest for a couple of hours. Only milk foods, with the additions of calcium lactate and the aforesaid glucose and honey, should be given for the first twenty-four hours, but after that if the temperature is nearly normal she will be ready for a small helping of finely chopped meat. From that time onwards, all being well, she will quickly get back to a regular routine of three milk meals and two meat meals alternating, ending the day with a last bowl of milk. If she refuses her food or eats and then vomits it up, take her temperature. The normal temperature of any dog is 101½° F. but it often rises a day after whelping to 102° F. or half a degree more without there being anything really wrong. However, if you are unhappy about the bitch do not delay but send for your veterinary surgeon, who will almost certainly give her an antibiotic injection.

The more quickly any upsets, however small, are attended to the better. If the bitch is making a good recovery she should be encouraged to go outside three or four times a day for a little exercise and to attend to the needs of nature. The first few times she may have to be lifted out of her box and carried outside as she will be reluctant to leave the puppies. At least once a day, for the first few days, it is usually necessary to get a bowl of warm water and Dettol to wash her tail and rear end, as there will be a little discharge that soon becomes unpleasant if neglected. See that she is well dried before returning her to her puppies. The removal of the dew claws is only a minor job and should be done before the puppies are a week old. An experienced breeder will attend to this herself but if you are not too sure about how to go about it get your veterinary surgeon to do it for you. It takes only a few minutes to attend to an ordinary sized litter.

Check over each puppy each day to see that the mother is keeping tails nicely washed and clean. If you do have to remove any dried excreta from their little behinds it is best to use warm olive oil to soften it, using a piece of cotton-wool.

The eyes will open at about two weeks, and the ears, gradually, a day or two later. From now on, with care and attention, regular feed times for the mother and the puppies, and a bed changed every day, there should be nothing to worry about. To have happy, healthy litters to watch over is one of the pleasantest pastimes I know.

American Ch. Rachelwood Raven, 1964

English and Australian Ch. Busybody of Branston, 1963

B. Thurse

Swedish Ch. Benefactor of Branston, 1965

B. Thurse

Ch. Quakertown Quistador, 1965

6

Puppy Rearing

THE importance of the way in which puppies are reared cannot be over-emphasised. Good conditions of housing and feeding are absolutely vital, and no detail unimportant or too much trouble; indeed, the true dog lover will spare no effort to see that puppies have as near perfect attention as possible. It is not good sense to neglect any aspect, at any age, when rearing puppies if one wishes to produce the best. This means not only puppies that are structurally sound with good pedigrees but also strong in bone and body and with good temperaments. The first essentials are a warm, dry, clean bed without draughts and sufficient food in small quantities at frequent intervals. Contented puppies are thriving puppies and, if their mother has amply supplied them with her own milk, at three weeks they should be nicely round and firm with their eyes and ears open and beginning to walk somewhat unsteadily around their bed. Remember to keep their toe nails cut very short, as by now they can be very long and sharp, and nothing tends to make their mother more irritable than little sharp claws working on her tummy while they take their nourishment.

Now is the time to offer them their first saucer of milk. It is advisable to use a fortified milk such as Lactol or a baby food such as Ostermilk; ordinary cow's milk is not rich enough, but if goat's milk is available there is nothing better. Whichever milk is used it should have a little honey or glucose added, and it should always be offered to them just warm. Nothing puts puppies off more than being offered cold milk. A saucer or shallow dish of milk held in one hand should be used, and the puppy steadied with the other hand. Directly their noses make contact with the dish they speedily get the idea and are ready for a drink. Sometimes they have already had a taste from their

E

mother's bowl of milk, the noise she makes when lapping enticing them to push their noses in to sample it.

For most of the third week of their lives two milk meals a day will be sufficient as they should still be getting the major part of their sustenance from their mother. However, at about four weeks, or when they appear slightly hungry, offer them half a teaspoonful of finely scraped raw meat. The preparation of this meat is rather a tedious job but is well worth it as only the juices and none of the fibres of the meat are given. The best way to do it is to cut a thick slice of good lean beef and then, with a strong sharp knife, scrape the meat until sufficient has been obtained. Take the puppies separately and offer the meat to them individually so that each has the correct amount.

Every few days the number of meals and the quantity given should be stepped up as they get more independent of their mother. By five weeks they will have arrived at five meals a day, which will now also include one of scrambled egg and one of minced cooked meat with broth. At six weeks a little Saval No. 2, scalded with the broth, can be added to the cooked minced meat meal and the raw meat meal can now be minced instead of scraped.

The following diet from seven weeks onwards, with variations, is usually satisfactory.

Diet Sheet

8 a.m. Warm milk (either Lactol, Ostermilk or goat's milk) with honey or glucose, fortified with Farex or Complan or
milk and raw egg beaten, or
lightly scrambled egg, or
rice crispies and milk.

11 a.m. Raw minced meat.

2 p.m. Warm milk with Farex and honey or any one of the alternatives of the 8 a.m. feed.

5 p.m. Minced warm cooked meat added to Saval No. 2, scalded with broth.

10 p.m. Good dish of warm milk and Farex with honey or sugar.

From about seven weeks it is best to give each puppy its own dish, but it is necessary to remain with them to see that they all eat from their own dish. Once they have eaten all they require remove the dishes otherwise they will soon have them turned upside down and the remains of the food on the floor.

Puppies love to have something to push around so give them a tightly sealed tin containing a few pebbles, which makes a most intriguing noise and gives endless enjoyment.

At five weeks it is time to let the bitch spend increasingly longer periods away from her puppies during the day. When the little sharp teeth start to come through the gums the dam soon becomes very weary of their perpetual demands. For at least another week the bitch should be left with them at night, but it is a good plan to devise somewhere where she can rest out of their reach if she desires.

Unless the weather is unusually warm they will still require a little artificial heat and it is, therefore, not necessary for the mother to sleep in the bed all the time.

At seven weeks the mother can be released from any further responsibilities for her litter but for several days she will probably demand to go back to them just to make certain they are safe and well. If she is taken back after her evening meal she will often regurgitate her food for them. This is quite natural; it contains some of her gastric juices, but it can be highly dangerous if she has been fed on large pieces of meat or paunch. The puppies will eagerly devour it if given the opportunity, but if these are large pieces they can get stuck in their throats, with unfortunate results. Therefore, if the bitch insists on returning to see her puppies once a day, it is better that she does so before her main meal or, alternatively, is fed on minced food.

Regarding training them to clean habits, the first lesson will start when they are about three weeks old and beginning to move around their bed. At this age a puppy instinctively tries to leave its bed to attend to the demands of nature but the high front to the box, fashioned to prevent them from falling out, also prevents them from walking out. Now is the time to change to a box without a front, so that they can easily walk out to attend to their needs and get back again. When they first start to leave their nest they should have only a fairly small area to move round in, for if they are at liberty to get too far from the box in their first venturings abroad they may get lost, stay at the far end of the kennel, and get chilled; nor should they be able to squeeze behind the box. If the space outside the box is limited to an area of about two yards, say for a week, they will soon get their bearings and then the space can be increased. This is quite easily contrived by fitting a 6-inch-wide piece of timber of required length across the kennel, a yard or so in front of the box. The arrangement also enables the mother to take her meals in peace, and prevents them from getting to her food.

The best floor covering is several thicknesses of newspaper, for which purpose every newspaper that comes into the house should be saved, also any that can be obtained from friends or neighbours. Whenever one goes into the kennel it is easy to pick up soiled papers and replace them with clean ones. It is surprising how quickly puppies choose one particular corner for toilet routine, leaving the rest quite unsoiled.

At this stage, when the dam has just left the puppies, it is very necessary to keep a watchful eye on their posteriors to see that they are managing to keep themselves clean. It is advisable to keep the hair round the anus cut very short, but in any case it should be examined every day, which also serves the dual purpose of getting puppies used to being handled by humans. Always hold the puppy firmly when picking it up so that it feels secure, and be sure that the hands are on the outside and never underneath the elbows, as nothing is more likely to ruin what would normally be a good straight front than wrong handling. Picking up puppies the wrong way and allowing them to go up and down steps at an early age are both equally disastrous.

Absolute cleanliness is another most important factor, not only feeding and drinking dishes but also the bedding. The bedding, whether of blankets or a sack thinly filled with hay, should be changed daily. It is a good practice to have a spare box available so that a fresh box with new bedding can replace the used one, which can then be scrubbed and dried ready for the next change. The same applies to having a spare kennel. To be able to remove a litter into a freshly clean kennel while the used one has a day for scrubbing and airing is ideal, and alternating from one to the other allows a far better chance for thorough cleaning, scrubbing and drying.

Whether the puppies appear to have worms or not, it is better to worm them at six weeks, at the latest.

It is far safest to ask your veterinary surgeon for reliable worming pills as he will supply the correct tablets for age and weight. The modern brands are very good and never distress or upset a puppy as they did in years gone by when very drastic medicines were used and puppies were starved for 24 hours before dosing. Today it is just a routine job, essential but not at all upsetting, if instructions are closely followed. Whether they turn out worms or not they always seem to be all the better for the treatment and appear to thrive.

At about six weeks, if the puppies are fortunate to be born in the spring or early summer, it is very good for them to be allowed out for short periods of play, preferably on a lawn or in a sheltered place, as soon as the weather is warm enough. Directly they show signs of tiring—probably in about half an hour—they should be returned to their kennel to sleep. Of course, in an uncertain climate great care must be taken to see that they are not put out in a cool wind or at any time when they could get chilled. They will soon be protesting loudly when they are returned to their kennel earlier than they think necessary.

Winter puppies are, of course, a more difficult problem. They still need a change of scene, and it is often easiest to take them into the house kitchen to play around, first having taken the precaution of removing all mats, shoes or brushes and anything too valuable for chewing. The more puppies are accustomed to strange noises the friendlier they will be. Puppies left too long in a kennel soon become shy and difficult. This extra attention takes up a lot of time but is well worth all the trouble in the long run.

It seems no time at all before they are eight weeks old, when serious thought must be given to which is to be kept or parted with. Eight to ten weeks is a good age to dispose of the first ones, but no puppy should be sold before it has reached the age of eight weeks.

It should be possible, when selling a puppy, to give a guarantee that it has been wormed twice at an interval of two weeks and that it is satisfactorily eating good solid food. Always give a written diet sheet to the new owner so that any sudden change of food which might upset the stomach is avoided.

Impress very strongly on the buyer the virtues of having the puppy fully inoculated directly it is three months old. Fortunately these precautions seem, nowadays, to be generally accepted, though there are still a few people who are prepared to risk a puppy's life rather than go to any extra trouble or expense. Such people should not be allowed to own a puppy. Anyone that has ever seen the misery of a dog with hardpad or distemper would have to have a heart of stone to withhold the protection afforded these days by the simple inoculation against these horrible diseases.

At the age of ten weeks puppies often seem to become bored with milk and minced food and one has to think out ways of getting them to take milk in various forms. A good helping of creamy rice pudding is acceptable occasionally, and finely cut up meat is more readily taken than the minced meat they have been having up to now. They are trying to show that they are past the age of baby foods and want something more solid, for they certainly seem to prefer their food served up nearly dry. At this age I have known them to eat slices of brown bread and butter, cut into small pieces, most readily. (Most puppies would win a prize for telling the difference between butter and margarine.) Whenever anything that is good and wholesome can be thought up let them have it for a change.

As they get older, using discretion, the number of meals may be reduced, first by stopping the 2 p.m. milk feed. The two meat meals, however, should always be increased in quantity as the various minor meals are omitted. Meat must always be the staple diet, with a suitable amount of biscuit.

At three months they will enjoy a hard biscuit such as Bonio to chew, and a whole marrow bone to gnaw at is beneficial in many respects. It will keep them occupied for hours, and even puppies will make a hole in a bone to get at the marrow, which they adore and which is very good for them. When they get to about four months old and are about to start losing their baby teeth, the bone will play an important part in loosening the milk teeth and helping the adult teeth through the gums. At this time the mouth should be examined every day to see that all is well. Sometimes the canines, which are the tusks at the sides, prove rather stubborn, and some assistance may be required to get them out before the second set of canines are through. This is highly important, otherwise the second teeth may be misplaced and a bad mouth result. Firmly pressing the thumb against each tooth several times a day will help loosen them without upsetting the puppy.

Nothing can be more heart-breaking than to have a superb puppy whose mouth does not reach the required degree of perfection, i.e. one whose jaw is either undershot or overshot or with very tiny misplaced incisors. Almost every breeder has, in their time, had to make the decision to sell as a pet a puppy that, up to about four months, seemed to be all that could be desired, but whose teeth have developed blemishes. A kennel run for show purposes must be absolutely ruthless in parting with any animal whose mouth is not up to the required standard. Some minor faults may be forgiven but a dog with an imperfect jaw or teeth will never be passed by a good judge, and to be tempted to breed from it is to risk perpetuating the fault for generations to come.

At about 12 to 14 weeks of age the puppies should be introduced to collar and lead, and once again all the patience that can be mustered is required. It should be possible to train a puppy to the lead without any show of force whatever. Using a very soft collar it is enough at first to let the puppy get used to the feel of it around its neck and then to trail it on the lead for five or ten minutes at a time. The handler should then pick up the lead and coax the puppy to follow a tit-bit or toy; cajole but never force. Once a puppy starts to struggle against the lead it is worse than useless to pull it about; the puppy only becomes frightened.

Some puppies will go easily at once whilst others may take days or even longer before capitulating. These first training sessions should always be brief and the puppy must never be overtired. Ideally, a lawn is better than a road. Once the puppy has learned its first lesson of going in the same direction as the handler, all that is required for several weeks more is a few minutes each day. It is still too young to be taken on the road for anything resembling a walk. In any event before the puppy makes its début on the public highway it should have had its full inoculations.

When the inoculations are completed it is time to introduce the puppy to the car, and the sooner the better. A puppy that is accustomed to short rides from its early days is less likely to be a bad traveller. It is very tiresome when travelling long distances to shows to have to take a dog that is habitually sick.

Another little lesson the puppy should learn in the first few months is to rest quietly in a travelling box.

I have found that for purposes of house training it is far easier if the puppy is shut in a travelling box at night. A puppy will rarely soil its own bed if it has been taken outside last thing at night, before its owner retires, and is carried outside immediately on rising in the morning. As soon as the puppy has become habitually clean at night it is no longer necessary to close the door of the box.

A well-trained puppy is a credit to its owner and ready to be accepted into society.

7

Trimming

THE art of trimming a West Highland White Terrier is not
acquired easily. On the tenacity of purpose of the owner
depends whether the complete mastery of the job is achieved in
one year or several. With some people it presents no problems,
and with a little guidance from a few friendly experts some
make a pretty good job of a show trim in a very short period. A
few, however, lack the necessary patience or real interest and
would rather leave the job to others.

To the real enthusiast, bringing a coat to perfection at the
right time for a show or shows is one of the more fascinating
aspects of preparing his dog. It is not a chore that is just
endured but a task to which the owner or handler gives much
time and thought before deciding to trim or even to remove just
a few hairs. Coats vary a good deal from dog to dog, and it is
only by studying each individual coat and treating it accordingly that the best effect will finally be achieved at the desired
time. It is not a thing anyone can just learn in a few lessons;
real determination to compete with the best has to be there.

From the time that the young puppy has its first tidy up to
the moment it is taken into the ring in all its glory at its first
show, every art that the expert knows has been used to achieve
near-perfect presentation.

When a West Highland White Terrier is finally prepared for
show it should look smart and neat but without any obvious
signs of having been trimmed. It should have a certain rugged-
ness, and no attempt must be made to make him look like a
Wire Fox Terrier.

A few newcomers to the breed sometimes make the mistake
of overtrimming, especially with clippers down the neck, which
is quite the wrong approach to the trimming of a Westie.

Various assortments of tools can be bought and are useful but the best tools of all are the fingers and good strong finger nails. Though, of course, there must be an assortment of cherished tools, among them a trimming knife with serrated edge will be most in use, a good quality pair of thinning scissors and ordinary scissors, and a favourite brush and comb.

Trimming hair by hair with finger and thumb will achieve better results than all the knives and scissors available. It is an art too rarely practised in these days. A scissored and clipped Westie is really offensive in the eyes of those who, over many years, have taken the trouble to trim and care for the coats correctly.

A puppy should have its first tidy up, hardly a trim, at about 3½ to 4 months old. All that is required is to remove, gently but firmly, the baby fluff, which by then is beginning to stand out and make the puppy look untidy. It will be found that underneath this first baby hair is a good new straight coat. This first trim makes a vast amount of difference to the puppy's appearance and it is easier to assess its good points when the fluff is removed.

The best method at this stage is to remove the hair all over with finger and thumb. It is usually quite easy to do this with a quick plucking action, taking only a few hairs at a time. Start just behind the head, and work along the back and down the sides, then the ears. If the puppy objects at all it will be when the more tender parts are reached, such as under the neck and down the chest. Here it is quite permissible to use thinning scissors, but it should be stressed that ordinary scissors mustnot be used, otherwise the puppy will end up with steps and ridges in its coat. Use the thinning scissors also down its hindquarters, as plucking here, too, can be very painful. The tail can be shaped up with either thinning scissors or knife.

It is a great mistake to neglect or defer this first trim too long, because afterwards the new coat comes on much more quickly. There only remains a slight tidying up of the legs and feet. Shape round the feet just a little without being too severe.

Great care must be taken at all times to avoid hurting or upsetting puppies when trimming; they have good memories and will remember for a long time if they have been hurt, and fear going on the trimming bench. Never let the puppy lose confidence in you, hold it firmly, and never let it fall or jump off the table.

After this initial trim all that is needed for some weeks is a light daily brushing and combing. The top half of the ears should be kept free of long hairs by finger and thumb plucking every week or so. The tail also needs to be kept well shaped by keeping the hair short and thick. Attend to the nails, if necessary. If they are always kept short the quick does not grow long and it is easy to keep the feet neat and tidy. Keep a good pair of nail cutters especially for that purpose. Nail cutters have short curved blades which fit over the nail. They are an essential piece of equipment because it is impossible to cut a dog's toe nails with ordinary scissors.

All these little attentions should be a matter of routine which, if carried out carefully, the puppies will look forward to because of the extra attention and handling they get.

If it is planned to show a dog at the age of about nine months, it is not too early to start the first trimming preparations at between six and seven months. A diagram for trimming an adult dog is included at the end of this chapter.

Always give the dog a thorough cleaning with Bob Martin's Clensfur or a good white chalk, brush and rub it thoroughly into the coat, allow the dog to have a good shake, and then comb well all over to remove every last tangle. It is always easier to trim after the coat has been chalked because one gets a better grip on the hair.

Whether using the finger or thumb method or a trimming knife, start behind the head and work down the neck, along the back and down the sides, removing any loose hair. The neck is more closely trimmed than the rest of the dog, and it is often necessary to resort to the use of thinning scissors under the throat and down the chest, but at this stage it is unwise to trim too closely. It is far better to do a little every week so that the coat becomes close and tight and gives the neck a shapely appearance. The trimming is continued down the shoulders to a slightly less degree so that it tapers off into the longer body hair without any obvious change from the fairly closely

trimmed neck hair to the body hair. This is often more difficult
to achieve than it sounds, but it is the persistent attention to
the coat over many weeks that gets the best results. The inexperienced owner will sometimes try to manage in a couple of
days what a wiser one will have been aiming at for weeks.
Remove some of the hair from the sides, for tidying up purposes, but I do not advocate the modern trend that seems to be
creeping in of removing most of the hair from the sides and
leaving a huge frill underneath the body. This type of trimming is probably designed to encourage the belief that the dog
has extra depth of body and flattish sides, but if the dog is
unfortunate enough to have barrel-shaped ribs a good judge
will not be deceived by the trimming, however craftily done.
Naturally, everyone aims to make the best possible presentation of the dog being shown, but a good judge is seldom
fooled.

The trimming of the front legs and elbows needs to be
tackled with some care. If the hair is very long it should be
slightly shortened; just taking off the tips of the straggly hair
helps it to grow thick and bushy and thus improves the
appearance of the legs. The tufty bits on the elbows must be
thinned back so that when standing in front of the dog the
elbows seem to lie snugly against the body. A little thinning
of the hair at the top of the outside of the foreleg will also
improve appearance. The feather on the back of the leg from
pastern to the elbow should be neatened, and the hair around
the front of the foot trimmed with scissors to make a tight
round foot. One pitfall to be avoided is to trim too closely
round the outside edge of the foot. This accentuates the
ankles and makes the feet appear to turn out, which is a bad
fault.

It is quite a fascinating job trying to trim a front to one's
entire satisfaction; a few hairs off here and there can make all
the difference to the final result. It is, however, very easy to
remove too much hair and regret it later, for there is no going
back, at least not for a good many weeks. Hair grows very
slowly on the legs, so it behoves one to trim them with very
great care.

The neatness of the foot is enhanced by well-kept nails. If the dogs are kept on concrete or brick runs their nails rarely need more than an occasional rub with a sharp file, but if their exercising is done entirely on grass the nails need to be watched carefully and cut and filed at regular intervals.

The back legs are trimmed on similar lines. Good thick hair on the hindquarters is a great asset and, again, only the tips of the hair are removed. Use the thinning scissors to get a neat close trim on the hindquarters but do not trim the hair between the legs too closely. Shorten the hair to a good shape on the hocks so that the dog looks right on his toes. It is essential to know, and admit to yourself at least, any faults your dog may have and trim accordingly. If the dog moves too closely behind, remove more hair from the inside of each back leg, the reverse of course applying if it moves too wide, when if more hair is left it will help to camouflage the fault.

If the hair on the head is rather thin and straggly at six months or so it is well to shorten it fairly drastically. The appearance will be spoilt temporarily but the benefit to the head will show in a month or two when the hair will have grown close and thick. A well-furnished head greatly improves appearance. Until recently many people used to leave a ruff standing out around the head, but it is rarely seen now. The cutting back of this ruff gives a better neck line and is more in keeping with the modern type of trimming.

By now the youngster should begin to look very smart, with a coat that is well shaped but without appearing to be over-trimmed. It is unlikely to have the depth and density of coat that will be acquired in later months, but once having shaped the neck and shoulders all that is needed is constant removal of any hair that begins to look loose. The coat should never be allowed to get untidy again. As every month passes, it will improve until at about nine or ten months, or according to how quickly the dog has matured, it will be ready to make its first appearance in the show ring. The occasional show will give the needed experience so that by the time it reaches the higher classes it will have a completely sophisticated look.

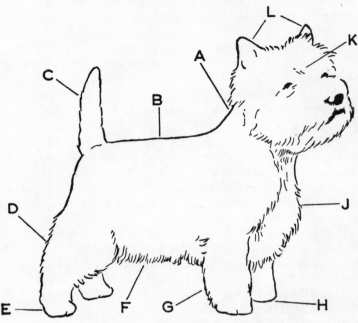

FIG. 5. TRIMMING CHART

A. Starting just behind the head, remove the untidy hair until there is a fairly tight top coat. Use the trimming knife or, if you are clever enough, the finger and thumb, a method that is less likely to damage the coat.

B. Continue this along the back and, to a lesser degree, down the sides. Taper the trimming of the neck and shoulders into the body coat.

C. Trim the tail so that it is thick at the base, tapering it to a point and leaving no feather hanging down the back of the tail.

D. Next, carefully tidy up the long hair over the back legs, being careful not to remove too much or, on the other hand, to leave big baggy pants. A Westie's legs should not have the same appearance as a Sealyham's back legs or a cowboy wearing chaps—this is seen too often.

E. Now get the feet in nice shape. The hair should be short and thick and well neatened all round.

F. Leave the skirt deep and full, only removing straggly hairs that may spoil the appearance.

G. Do not remove the feather on the back of the front legs but even up any untidy ends.

H. Tidy around the front feet and see that the nails are short, using nail clippers and a file if necessary.

J. Tidy under the neck. It is nearly always necessary to use thinning scissors here because the neck is a very tender part on most dogs.

K. The head furnishings should be thick and full. Just even up the ruff to make a good frame for the face.

L. Remove the long hairs from the ears with finger and thumb, gently but firmly, with quick plucking movements until the top half of the ear is smooth and velvety. The hair on the lower half of the ear should *not* be removed but allowed to blend into the head furnishings.

A well-turned-out West Highland White Terrier should look smart without appearing to be trimmed, showing a good neck and shoulders and body shape, and not being shaved in some parts and ridiculously over-furnished in others.

It is essential at all times to keep in mind the points shown in the Standard of the Breed.

8

Preparation for Show

WHETHER you start showing activities with a puppy or a young dog it is necessary to allow plenty of time in which to prepare it in every way. The training or education may sometimes be completed in a few weeks but some dogs require months before they have gained the necessary confidence that will ensure their making the best of themselves when they appear for the first time in the ring.

So much depends on the amount of attention that has been given to the puppy from babyhood. If it has spent a lot of time with the family in the house and learned to meet strangers without any sign of nervousness or shyness then the task is much easier. A puppy that has had completely happy surroundings all its short life is hardly ever dismayed by unusual happenings and is likely to be a natural showman and need very little extra training for its first outing to a show. If a dog has been kept exclusively in a kennel, however, even with plenty of companions of its own kind, it will be a great ordeal the first time it has to meet strangers, and you may have to concentrate all your efforts and exercise a great deal of patience before it responds as well as you could wish.

If you are to have a six-months-old puppy ready to show by the time it is nine or ten months old there is no time to be lost in making preparations for the great day. Conditioning, grooming, and training, all should be a daily occurrence. Give the dog as much attention as possible so that it really feels important. Always be consistent in your training programme so that the puppy will quickly know what to expect. The whole time spent in training should be a pleasure to which both you and the puppy look forward each day. Keep the puppy happy and it will want to please you.

Ch. Pillerton Peterman, 1966

Anne Roslin-Williams

Ch. Lasara Louise, 1967

C. M. Cooke

Mrs C. Pacey judging Ch. Brenda of Branston
and Ch. Sollersot Soloist

Anne Roslin-Williams

Ch. Checkbar Donsi Kythe, 1969

First is the daily grooming on the table, after which you will persuade it to stand quietly, posed in a correct but easy manner. After a few lessons an adaptable dog will soon learn that you wish it to remain in the same position for a while. While it is so posed go over the dog with your hands, as a judge will do, feeling its head, neck and shoulders, and particularly its feet as some dogs dislike their feet touched. Look at its teeth each day so that it becomes just routine and there will be no fuss or nonsense when the judge wishes to see its teeth. More than one dog has been known to throw away its chances of a prize by refusing to let the judge handle its mouth. Next comes a short daily lesson in walking and standing. Use the same sort of lead that you will use when showing the dog. With the lead in your left hand, walk the dog at a fairly smart but comfortable speed. Restrict the length of your walk before turning about twenty yards from your starting point, the average length of a show ring. Move the dog back and forth across the imagined ring several times. Then make a circular tour, still with the lead in your left hand. At frequent intervals stop and speak encouragingly and gain its attention so that it stands looking towards you in an expectant manner. This is the time to reward it with a piece of liver or some other tit-bit that you have concealed in your pocket. If the liver is kept in a piece of paper that rustles the dog will soon connect the sound with the liver it hopes to receive. Try to get the dog used to moving on a fairly loose lead and to walk close by your side. Stop before you feel that the dog is becoming bored. Always try to keep the dog interested and bright. The very tone of your voice can be important. If you are bored, the dog will be too. It is better to have short sessions twice a day than longer periods. Don't give up in despair if the dog seems to be responding more slowly than you had hoped. There are very few dogs that cannot be trained with patience and kindness. Always praise your dog when it has behaved well.

Once the dog is really responding to its training seek the co-operation of your family and a few friends. If you can muster half a dozen people, and their dogs, you can have the semblance of a private dog show. Someone can be asked to

F

play the role of judge while others take all available dogs, mongrel or otherwise, round the ring. This introduces your dog to the niceties of good behaviour and will stop it from being anti-social when it gets to its first show. It is a good thing for the dog to show a lively interest in the other dogs without wanting to fight them. It gives a wrong image of West Highlands as a whole if some seem to be looking for a fight all the time. Unfortunately, it is thought by some that a terrier lacks spirit if it is not trying to get involved in fights but, of course, this is not so. West Highlands are friendly creatures and usually greet other dogs in an interested but amiable manner.

It is a good thing to accustom all dogs to a travelling box. Some may always be able to travel loose in a car to a show but there are many more that travel in boxes. If they are accustomed to a box they make no fuss and travel comfortably and happily. Start by shutting the dog in its travelling box at home for half an hour at a time. When it finds that it is to be let out again it soon loses all fear of being shut in for longer periods. Dogs should not be kept in cages or boxes for longer than is absolutely essential, but they should be trained to accept it for short periods so that if they must be boxed for any reason they do not become distressed. The box should be large enough for the dog to be able to turn round in it easily and high enough for it to be able to stand up. Ventilation is vitally important. There should be plenty of air holes that cannot in any circumstances get covered up to stop the air circulating freely.

While all this training is going on constant attention to the coat must be maintained, as explained in Chapter 7. At about six months, having kept the dog's coat reasonably tidy and well shaped, all that should be necessary is to give it daily grooming and some trimming, preferably by the finger and thumb method. It is better to keep at it every day since this does away with long hours of preparation on the last day or so before the show and it produces the desired result more easily and painlessly. Constantly plucking away hairs that are loose and spoil the outline will keep the coat tight for an almost indefinite length of time. Pluck any long hairs off the top half of the ears, which should be kept really smooth, and always pluck with the finger and thumb. The back and sides of the neck and the shoulders also need frequent attention. About once a week lightly use the thinning scissors under the throat to keep the hair short and tight. The top of the body and partially down the sides can be kept neat and tidy if a little is removed every day or so, as necessary. If this programme is maintained for three months prior to its first show in the last two or three days only the final finishing off will be needed: the shaping of the tail, a little neatening round the feet, and the removal of any surplus hair.

See that the teeth are clean. Sticks for removing tartar can be obtained from most chemists and are quite simple to use. Examine the toe nails and, if necessary, cut and file them with a coarse file.

During all this period of training and grooming and trimming the dog must be kept in perfect health and condition. A dog that is not enjoying its food can go out of condition and lose body very quickly. The diet must be balanced, and the food fresh and of the best quality so that it is eaten with relish; for if the dog is not in top physical condition it will not make the most of itself. Good regular food is essential: plenty of meat twice a day and a small quantity of best biscuit. An egg beaten up in milk three or four times a week is appreciated by most dogs and seems to put that little extra zip into them. The meals should be well spaced out and all food dishes removed directly they are empty. Do not over-feed, otherwise the dog will sicken of food and have a stomach upset, the last thing that should be allowed to happen a few days before a show. If the dog becomes bored, keep it on a light diet for a day or two and, at the same time, give it a condition powder each day. This should bring it back into sparkling form quickly. Each dog needs to be treated as an individual, for what suits one does not always suit another. Some will thoroughly enjoy grated carrot and chopped greens mixed with their main meal, but others will sort out all vegetables, however carefully they are mixed in with the meat and biscuit.

Every dog should have at least one complete spell of freedom each day, weather permitting. A dog can cover a lot of ground in fifteen minutes, so whenever possible let the dog out for exercise directly the kennel doors are open. That quick scamper round the garden will liven up the circulation, induce the bowels to move, and give the dog an opportunity of visiting his favourite haunts to see if there is a rabbit waiting to be chased or a mole to be dug out. In bad weather, this very enjoyable exercise may naturally have to be restricted or curtailed altogether, especially just before the show.

Having brought the dog to the peak of condition all that is left is the final clean up. This must be very thorough. Start by washing the stomach, legs and feet and, lastly, the head. Do not wash the dog all over or the hair on the top of the back may become unmanageable. When the dog is dried, finish off by well rubbing all over with chalk; then use brush and comb. When the dog has had a shake and is combed down again you can see if there are any last bits of hair that need to be removed. Never think that you can get away with half cleaning a West Highland; it will stand out a mile if you have not done the job properly.

If the show is a long distance away it will probably be necessary to make an early start, so have everything packed overnight. A capacious holdall will be required to pack all the things that will be needed, which will not be just a brush and comb to tidy the exhibit at the last minute. Once you have seen exhibitors staggering into shows laden with bags, stools, folding table, and everything else that seems necessary for a stay of from six to eight hours, you will soon realise more will be required than those two indispensable items. It is safest to make a list of things that will be needed, and it will be a long one. Bench blankets, bench chains, a tin of cleaning powder, scissors, thinning scissors, trimming knife, all may be needed in case, even at this late hour, a little more trimming is found necessary. Besides these there should be a polythene bottle of water for the dog, and a substantial helping of meat, for it will be a long day, and the dog deserves sustenance as much as its owner. Having made sure that everything the dog needs has been packed, if there is a little room left take a big thermos flask of coffee and a packet of sandwiches for yourself. Beyond that there is no limit to the bits and pieces that you may decide to take along 'just in case': another pair of stockings to replace those you may spoil if you unfortunately fall over a tent-peg, perhaps another pair of comfortable shoes, and toilet requisites for freshening up at the end of the day. There is no end to the list, but it is all part of the fun of getting ready for another dog show.

9

Exhibiting

To have a good dog to show, one that has been bred and reared, trained and prepared by the owner, is one of the most satisfying experiences known to any breeder of dogs. Even if the dog is not destined to reach top honours, the thrill of matching it time and again against some of the top dogs, with varying degrees of success at successive shows, can be highly stimulating. Inevitably, every owner, in the security of its home surroundings, thinks that his own dog is a winner, but there is only one way to have that judgement confirmed, and that is to put it in open competition against others of its kind.

There are four grades or types of shows, which are:

(a) Sanction Shows, open only to members of the society promoting the show and restricted to twenty-five classes. It is unbenched.

(b) Limited Shows, also restricted to members, with a maximum of sixty-five classes and usually unbenched.

(c) Open Shows, in which there are no restrictions on the number of classes and which are open to all, whether members or not. These are invariably benched shows. A breed society is, however, permitted, to hold an unbenched Open Show restricted to twenty classes.

(d) Championship Shows. These are similar to Open Shows except that Kennel Club Challenge Ceritficates are offered. They are always benched and offer bigger prize money.

It is as well for any intending exhibitor to have visited at least one or more shows to gain some elementary knowledge of what will be expected of her when she makes her début with her dog in the ring. Even if attending the show only as a spectator it is best to arrive in good time to watch all the preparations that each person is making before taking the dogs into the ring, but at this stage it is unwise to pester the exhibitors with all the questions that are begging to be asked. Dog people are always glad to help a beginner by giving them information, but not when they are intent on preparing their own dog for the ring. Save up all questions until judging is over, when they will get a much better reception, and the most helpful exhibitors may even be prepared to give a free demonstration in trimming and show preparation into the bargain. It is certainly time well spent to have visited one or two shows for the purpose of gaining an inkling of what is required, and show procedure, before venturing out to show a dog for the first time.

Before entering for a show the dog must be registered at the Kennel Club. All the current charges for registering, transfer fees, and so on are printed in Chapter 11.

Until becoming a fairly regular exhibitor at shows, it is necessary to write for schedules from the secretaries of the societies promoting shows that you feel would be a suitable one for starting a dog on its show career. When the schedule is received, read it thoroughly. Having made up your mind to enter the dog for a show it will be a bitter disappointment to find that the final date for entries closed a few days earlier. Secretaries are not permitted, by Kennel Club rules, to accept entries posted after the latest date stated in the schedule.

If you are showing a puppy for the first time it is best not to be too ambitious but to be content with an entry in a puppy class or if there is not a puppy class scheduled, then the next lower class.

Having made the entry, in due course, usually a few days before the show, a pass on which is the dog's number will be received from the secretary. It is essential to take this with you to the show, for without it your dog will not be admitted.

If the entry is for a championship show no effort will have been spared for weeks beforehand to have the dog trimmed to the last hair and in tip-top condition, but even so, the day before the show there is always that final overhaul to ensure that the dog is perfectly clean and looking as well turned out as possible. Even after attending shows for thirty years I still have that feeling of excitement and bustle on the last day as I pack all the necessary equipment to take to the show. Generally, it means an early night ready for setting out at the crack of dawn. Even dogs catch this undercurrent of excitement and are as eager to be up and off as their owners. Those that have been through all the ritual of preparation the day before give tongue directly they hear the first stirrings of the household. The final question before you are driving off is, 'Have we got the tickets?'.

Arriving early at the show gives many advantages. One is finding a handy parking site; another, getting inside the show before the vast throng of other exhibitors and their dogs arrive. (Veterinary inspection is no longer required.) Coping single-handed with a couple of dogs and a heavy bag containing all the paraphernalia that always seems so necessary makes early arrival at a show vitally important. Having found the bench allotted to your dog, and comfortably settled him, not forgetting to see that he is really securely chained on a chain that prevents him from getting too near the front of the bench, where he might fall off and hang himself, then it is time to relax a little. A bowl of cold water for the dog, and a hot cup of tea or coffee from the thermos flask for yourself, and you will feel like a giant refreshed. Before starting to groom the dog it is advisable to buy a catalogue and find out the number of the ring in which West Highlands are to be judged. If it is a very large show, do some reconnoitring so that you will know in advance how far you have to go from your bench to the ring. It is now time to get to work to remove any travel stains from the dog and to return him to the pristine freshness he had when he left home hours earlier. If he was thoroughly cleaned the previous day, probably only his legs and feet will be soiled, and a rub all over with a little chalk will bring back the shining whiteness. Because he has a white coat it is more than ever necessary that he should be absolutely clean. A half-clean Westie looks dreadful. Once he has been cleaned and well combed out return him to his bench and, settling him comfortably, leave him to rest without further interference until he is required to be taken to the ring. Until judging is over it is unwise ever to be far away. The order of judging may, for some reason or other, occasionally have to be changed. It is your responsibility to be ready and waiting so that when the call 'West Highlands in the ring' comes, you can at least appear to be cool, calm and collected even if your knees are knocking.

It is useful to have in the dress, smock or pants, or whatever is being worn at the time, a large pocket for a piece of liver or some other tempting tit-bit that the dog has been trained at home to expect as a reward for good behaviour. This can be surreptitiously offered to him as and when the need arises, to encourage him to show himself off. A small steel comb or brush carried in the pocket may also come in useful for smoothing down his coat. Sometimes the coat is disarranged by the time the judge has finished his examination, and to do justice to the dog any stray hairs should be slicked down with one or two strokes of the brush or comb.

Directly the stewards call for the first class, if your dog is entered in that class take him into the ring, where the steward will hand you your ring card, which should immediately be attached to some part of your clothing where it can be easily seen by everyone. Club members usually have club badges which are designed to hold the ring card, but failing this a small brooch or pin will suffice to hold the card in place. Once all the exhibits for that class are assembled in the ring the steward will direct the exhibitors to stand in an orderly fashion at one side of the ring and, when he is satisfied that everything is in order, he will tell the judge that all is ready for him. Do not wander about; stay where you have been placed until you are told to move either alone or collectively with the others.

If your dog is not entered in the first class, watch from the ringside to see how quickly judging is proceeding so that when the time comes for your class you will be ready to enter the ring without delay.

From the time you enter the ring concentrate all your attention on your dog. Be calm and self-assured, with confidence in your dog. A West Highland is by nature an assertive dog, ready to greet his nearest rival in an inquisitive manner. It is permissible to allow him to make friendly overtures to other exhibits but he should be restrained from becoming too boisterous or interfering with any dog that does not welcome his attentions. It is considered bad sportsmanship ever to allow one dog to upset another exhibitor's dog. Good manners in the show ring are as essential as in any other walk of life. If showing for the first time, try to place yourself well along the line so that the more experienced exhibitors come before the judge first. This will give you time to adapt yourself to what is going on and then, when your turn comes, you can follow their lead with confidence.

It is usual for the judge to request the exhibitors to go round the ring first. This gives the dogs a chance to settle down and, at the same time, the judge an opportunity for an overall survey of the dogs he is about to judge. Every judge has his own idiosyncrasies about how he likes dogs paraded and brought to him. Some prefer to see each dog move before handling; others want the dog on the table first, and then see its movements. Whatever method is adopted it is up to exhibitors to conform to the judge's directions to the best of their ability.

It is most usual in our breed for the judge to examine each dog on the table, therefore, as soon as the exhibitor preceding you lifts her dog off the table lift yours on to the table, and deftly pose it to the best advantage so that as the judge turns, having by now finished with the previous exhibit, his first impression of your dog is as favourable as you could wish. As the judge starts to examine the dog he will almost certainly ask you its age. Answer clearly and without elaborating in any way. The judge is not interested to know that this is your first show or that someone told you he ought easily to become a champion. Just stand quietly by, keeping your hands out of his way and not touching the dog more than is absolutely necessary.

When the judge is finished he will ask you to move the dog across the ring in a straight line away from him, and then to bring him back again. If he is not satisfied with his movement the first time, he may say 'take him again'. As good movement is so important in a terrier the judge will probably want to see a side view of his action. Never allow yourself to get between the judge and the dog, for however stylish a mover you may be, at that particular moment it is your dog's and not your movement he is concerned with. Always be aware of where the judge has placed himself so that if necessary you can quickly change the lead from the left to the right hand. When moving the dog let him go at the pace that suits him best and to which he has been accustomed when training at home, unless the judge asks you to move either more quickly or slowly. Most Westies like to move at a fairly brisk pace, and a good showman will go gaily and willingly without coaxing. It is best to show them on a fairly loose lead. To string them up on a tight lead is discouraged now far more than it was years back. The dog will move better and much more freely if the lead is loose. The lead should be held so that if any check is necessary the dog will respond immediately to the slightest tightening of the lead. When the judge is finished with you take your place next to the exhibitor that preceded you.

While the rest of the dogs are being seen let your dog relax a little but still remain aware of what the judge is doing, so that when he again turns to the dogs, by now lined up for his final appraisal, your dog is once more on his toes and showing himself to the best advantage to catch the judge's eye. So often, when a lot of good dogs are gathered together and there seems to be little between them, it is the last bit of showmanship that tells. If your dog recognises that tone of encouragement in your voice or hears the faint rustle of paper in your pocket, which indicates a piece of liver or some other tasty morsel coming his way, he may exert that last little extra effort that will make all the difference. If you are one of the few picked out for an award, move at once to the position indicated. Never relax for an instant until the judge has actually marked his book. Many a judge about to mark his book, has taken one last look and found an exhibitor allowing her dog to stand badly in an unguarded moment, thinking that it was all over, and then rearranged his placings.

If you are not among the first three and 'in the money', as the old hands call it, then accept the judge's decision gracefully and find a smile and a cheerful word of congratulation for the winners. Scowling at the judge will do no good to anyone, least of all yourself, and although you are convinced yours was the better dog the judge was probably less biased and saw faults that you were not even aware your dog possessed.

If you are in only one or two classes, return your dog to his bench directly he is finished with and then go back to the ring-side to watch the rest of the judging. Watching the more experienced perform is one of the best ways of learning the art of handling. You will see the effortless ease with which they take their dogs through their paces, the dogs seeming to know just what is required of them.

Listening to a group of knowledgeable people discussing the merits or failings of each dog in the ring can also be most revealing. There is so much to see and so much more to learn than the beginner can ever have imagined. There can be a life-time of the keenest pleasure in showing dogs if the right attitude to it is adopted at all times. Never let disappointments sour you, or success go to your head. It is invariably the lot of the most successful to have their share of reversals, but if you care more for the good of the breed than anything else you will take it all in your stride. Besides all else you will meet the nicest people from all walks of life, all brought together by their love of a good West Highland.

There are more professional handlers than ever before in the Westie rings, and many owners feel at a disadvantage when showing their own against these experts. This is wrong; it should be looked on as a challenge to prepare, and get as much out of, your exhibit as any handler. They know their job but it can be learnt by all. With attention to detail in preparation and an understanding of your dog's temperament nothing is impossible. Time and patience can achieve anything if you have a quality dog to work on. And what a sense of achievement proudly to take your own dog to the top despite the stiffest opposition.

10

Judging

To be invited to judge is a very great compliment and it is not a task to be lightly undertaken. A good judge must have enough confidence to make decisions that may not be too popular but which, on the day, seem right.

An apprenticeship of several years judging at Open Shows used, until recently, to be required by the Kennel Club before anyone could undertake to judge at a Championship Show, but this rule has now been partially relaxed in favour of proof of a breeder's or exhibitor's ability to breed champions and recognise good stock. Before judging a Championship Show the Kennel Club requires the would-be judge to complete a form stating the names and numbers of Champions bred or owned and a detailed summary of judging experience.

To the average person the first engagement to judge at a Championship Show is something of an ordeal. However, it is such an absorbing task that ringside spectators and their comments are soon forgotten.

Naturally, it is expected that the judge should be fully conversant with the standard of the breed, but as no two judges ever quite agree on what is perfection each show brings a fresh thrill or disappointment to some exhibitor.

The approach to judging should be serious, with a full realisation of the responsibility that is to be borne for that particular day. There should be no place for petty-mindedness, and personalities should have no influence on decisions made.

Always arrive in good time. It is not good manners to keep exhibitors waiting; they will have put in a lot of hard work, and travelled long distances, and they will be anxious to get on with the job. In the ring have a few words with your steward, who is a most important person. A good steward will keep everything moving smoothly so that the judge can concentrate solely on the job in hand. The steward will marshal the dogs in the ring, see that none are missing, and that they stand in an orderly manner as required.

Have a method and stick to it for every class so that everyone can be prepared when their turn arrives to be scrutinised.

Terriers always look at their best when moving, and it is as well, if the ring provided is large enough, to begin by having all the dogs move round the ring at a brisk pace. This gives an opportunity for a preliminary sizing up of the dogs and, at the same time, settles them down. Twice round the ring is sufficient; there is no need to keep it up until everyone is giddy.

Set to in a workmanlike manner with a clear mental picture of what you require. Systematically go over each dog in turn. It is the custom in the United Kingdom for a good firm table to be provided so that the dogs may be placed on it. It certainly looks more becoming for a judge to examine a dog while standing erect than almost on his or her knees. At the same time it gives a better view to the ringsiders for whom it can be most instructive in seeing the way each judge goes about his task.

The method by which a judge uses his hands in going over a dog often speaks louder than words. It is almost possible to see into a judge's mind and to know what he is searching for as his hands pass from one salient point to another: the beautiful layback of good shoulders, the quality of bone in the legs and the feet; weighing up a slightly doubtful mouth against the virtue of a good dark eye. Automatically the judge's mind takes it all in. Everything must be considered but, at the same time, his mind is searching for the type and quality he hopes to find. Sometimes it seems if one judged each dog solely on the allotted points, they *could* all be equal, but they never are. There is some indefinable quality in the best that makes one dog seem to stand out from all the rest. To award a Challenge Certificate and Best of Breed to a dog that completely satisfies you is something to remember. All judges must surely remember for ever the occasion when an outstanding dog came before them, and what a joy it was to handle that dog. Judging is not quite always so satisfying. There may be times when every dog in a class seems mediocre. It is far more difficult to sort out a poor class than several good ones.

If a judge is faced with a very large class it is better, after each dog has been thoroughly examined and the chances of the best dozen dogs estimated, to allow the remainder to leave the ring. It is less confusing than keeping all of them standing in uncertainty until the final awards are made. Try, if possible, to stick to type and size. If a judge knows his own mind he is not likely to select one that is very heavy bodied and low to ground and the next one high on the leg and quite the opposite in every way from the first. A judge must always be quite firm and definite in making decisions and not be in the least concerned about what the spectators are thinking. It is impossible to please everyone. Because a well known dog comes before you it is not enough to rely on its reputation as a big winner. Have a completely open mind, and if it does not come up to the high standard you expect and you can fault it, do not be influenced by what you know other judges have done. Neither should you seek sensationalism by putting down a good dog just to show that you can be different from everyone else.

Should a dog make a display of temper and refuse to have its mouth examined, a judge is quite justified in placing it in a very low position even though in every other respect it may be a very handsome creature. The same applies if the exhibit refuses to move freely. No matter how perfect it may look when posed by the handler, if it literally has to be dragged across the ring with its tail down it is not showing the characteristic temperament of the breed. The judge may be fully aware that that particular dog is as good a showman as any, on some occasions, but the dog must be judged on its performance on the day.

If one or two dogs take a dislike to each other and persist in trying to fight, the judge should insist that they are firmly controlled and not allowed to upset the rest of the class. The breed has a wonderful reputation for possessing good-tempered dogs, none should be allowed to destroy it.

Soundness of action is of very great importance. Without it no dog will ever move properly and a judge must therefore pay a good deal of attention to its action both going and coming.

Movement, indeed, is often the deciding factor between dogs of almost equal merit in other respects. A really stylish one will take the eye of the judge at once.

Always be most conscientious about giving the same amount of consideration to each dog; on no account give any exhibitor cause for feeling that his dog· has been neglected or overlooked. A judge should make clear-cut decisions without hesitation. Just as many, if not more, mistakes are made after weighty consideration than by the swift instinctive decision. When it is all over and you have done your best, never feel that you need apologise to anyone for having placed a dog in a more lowly position than was expected. If judging has been done as conscientiously as one knows how, there should be no reason to make excuses or justify one's placings. Any feeling of disappointment an exhibitor may momentarily feel is usually quickly dissipated as his natural good sportsmanship reasserts itself.

As in most things, judging has its lighter side, as I discovered a few years ago when judging a huge puppy class at Crufts. Deep in thought, and madly concentrating, I slowly became aware that the spectators round the ring seemed to be enjoying a great joke. Hardly daring to move I took a cautious look round. To my great relief I found that a group of pigeons had alighted close behind me and were taking a great interest in the proceedings, and the puppies were showing much animation as they strained at the ends of their leads in the hope of catching a tasty meal.

A judge should try to go about his task as efficiently as possible, remaining unflustered and quite calm at all times, and women judges in particular should be attired in something that allows them to move about in comfort and yet looks neat and tidy after much bending and stooping. Comments overheard from the ringside can be shattering as well as flattering. Skirts that are too tight or too short have been known to cause some amusement, and jangling beads and bracelets can be disturbing to the dogs. It is said that one smart female judge nearly lost her finger when a dog mistook her blood-red nails for a piece of steak.

Never fear criticism; be honest and conscientious, and all will respect you as a judge.

Ch. Cedarfell Merry N'Bright, 1970

Ch. Whitebriar Jonfair, 1971

Henry C. Schley

American Ch. Lymehills Birkfell Solstice, 1971

Wilhelm Dufwa

Int. and Nordic Ch. Tweed Tartan Maid, 1971

11

The Kennel Club

ALL shows, except Exemption, are held under Kennel Club Rules and Regulations, copies of which may be obtained from the Secretary of the Kennel Club.

Every dog entered for any show (except Exemption) must be registered, or if already registered when purchased must be transferred to the new owner at the Kennel Club. It is, however, permissible to enter a dog for a show if the Registration or Transfer Cards have not been received back from the Kennel Club by the time entries close, provided that application has been made before that time. In these cases the letters N.A.F. (name applied for) or T.A.F. (transfer applied for), as the case may be, are added after the selected name or registered name.

Registration, transfer forms, etc., may be obtained from The Secretary, The Kennel Club, 1–4 Clarges Street, Piccadilly, London, W1Y 8AB.

LIST OF THE VARIOUS FEES

	£	p
Registration by breeder	1	00
Registration by any person other than the breeder	2	50
Breeder's declaration not signed	2	50
Registration name not changeable (additional fee)	2	00
Re-registration	2	00
Transfer	1	00
Change of name	5	00
Registration of Affix	6	00

	£	P
Affix maintenance fee (annual)	2	00
Holders of affix may compound for 20 years on the payment of £15		
Pedigrees—three generations	5	00
five generations	7	50
export	10	00

The following Regulation was approved by the Kennel Club Show Regulations Committee in January 1961 and appeared in the *Kennel Gazette* in February 1961. It was subsequently incorporated in the Kennel Club Championship Show Regulations pamphlet B(1) as regulation 9(i):

'If an exhibitor reports before the judging of a class or classes that he has entered a dog which is ineligible—

(1) as regards its breed, colour, sex, weight or height the Show Secretary shall transfer it to the equivalent class or classes for the correct breed, colour, sex, weight or height and, in the event of there being no equivalent class, to the Open Class for the correct breed, colour, sex, weight or height.

(2) for any other reason other than above the Show Secretary shall transfer it to the Open Class.'

The Committee of the Kennel Club has agreed to endorse registration certificates on request by the owner, i.e. the person who makes the original registration, as follows:

NOT ELIGIBLE FOR EXPORT PEDIGREE

The endorsement can only be removed by the person who made the endorsement or requested it.

12

The Breed Overseas

EACH year the number of countries taking up the West Highland White Terrier increases. Distance presents no problem now that transport of livestock has become routine, and in most cases every consideration is given to the dogs' comfort. Now that the virtues of the breed are more fully recognised there seems to be no limit to the number of people determined to possess a. West Highland. From far-flung corners of the world enquiries come for, sometimes, just a good companion, but in most instances for a really first-rate dog or bitch to improve present stock or as a foundation for a new kennel.

United States of America

America has long made heavy demands on the breed in the British Isles and many of the best bred in the U.K. cross the water to continue their distinguished careers in other hands.

In so vast a country as the U.S.A., although incredible distances are travelled to the major shows, it is quite possible that some of the best may never meet in competition.

The West Highland White Terrier, when it was still known in America as the Roseneath terrier, was first scheduled at the Westminster Show in 1907, and two years later, in 1909, The West Highland White Terrier. Club of America was formed.

The first one of the breed to become an American champion was the English-bred Clonmel Cream of the Skies, bred by the famous Holland Buckley, one of the greatest authorities on the breed in the very early days.

The enthusiasm that is typical of our American friends is very infectious and they spare no effort, time or expense to breed and own the best possible. Many of the imports from Britain have gained the highest honours.

One of the earliest 'greats' to make history was surely the English-bred Ch. Ray of Rushmoor, bred by Miss Smith-Wood in June 1927 and later exported to Mrs John G. Winant, in whose famous Edgerstoune kennel he sired ten champions, all but one bearing the Edgerstoune prefix. Later, many of the best Wolvey champions bred by Mrs Pacey joined the Edgerstounes. Ch. Wolvey Pattern was the first West Highland to go Best in Show at Westminster, a great achievement of which his English breeder was justly proud.

Mrs R. K. Mellon, whose prefix 'Rachelwood' is attached to so many good home-bred Westies, has bred many champions and imported several others, first from the Wolvey kennels and, later, from the 'Hookwoods' owned by the then Miss Ella Wade, who supplied Ch. Hookwood Banneret and Ch. Hookwood Marquis. Still more recently my own kennel has sent out Ch. Bannock of Branston, Ch. Bavina of Branston and, the latest to go to the 'Rachelwoods', Ch. Bardel of Branston and Ch. Briar Rose of Branston.

Other stalwarts of the breed, Mrs Wm Worcester and her daughter Barbara, now Mrs Ed Keenan, have imported several English champions, the most famous and successful undoubtedly being Ch. Cruben Dextor. Dextor, in addition to being a spectacular showman, was also a great stud force, having sired a large number of champions. Mrs Sayers also imported the English-bred dog Elfinbrook Simon, who quickly qualified for his title, success culminating in his becoming the second West Highland to go Best in Show at Westminster, America's premier show.

It would be impossible to list all the names famous for breeding good West Highlands in that great country but a few that come readily to mind are Mr and Mrs John T. Marvin's 'Cranbournes', Mrs Brumby's 'Rannockdunes', Mrs Frame's 'Wigtowns', Mr and Mrs Edward Danks's 'Battisons', Mrs C. Fawcett's 'Forest Glen', and Mr and Mrs A. Walters's 'Tyndrum'. There are many, many others all playing their part in keeping the breed to the forefront of dogdom.

The export regulations for sending a dog to the United States of America are quite simple. All that is required is the export pedigree and a certificate of health from the local veterinary surgeon.

Canada

The beginning of the West Highland White Terrier in Canada is very obscure but one of the oldest breeders today must without doubt be Mr Victor Blochin of the Bencruachan Kennels, Ontario. His introduction to the breed was during the First World War when, as a young Russian officer, he was taken prisoner. Among his fellow prisoners was Angus Campbell of Dunstaffnage Castle, Scotland, who promised him one of his Westies when it was all over.

In 1922, after the Russian revolution, Mr Blochin came to Scotland and received from Angus Campbell a bitch, which he called Snejka, meaning Little White Snow Flake. When Mr Blochin went to Canada in 1927 he took with him a son of Snejka's, who sired many Bencruachans.

Mr Blochin imported from Miss I. R. Maclean Cowie Rowmore Ardifuir who, in addition to soon becoming a Canadian Champion, was the only West Highland White Terrier to become a Grand Champion, a Canadian award no longer given. It was obtained by winning, in addition to the ten points required for the title of Champion, a further ten points with only champions competing for it.

Mr Blochin has a cemetery for dogs where all their dogs are laid to rest, and for several years it has been open to all Canadian pets. Many well-known names may be seen on the stones.

The Bencruachan Kennels no longer do any exhibiting but they still breed a few litters and carry on the cemetery and boarding business.

Another old kennel is that of Miss Edith Humby and the late Miss Rosamond Billet whose Highland Kennel won their first Best in Show with Edgerstoune Stardust. In 1939 they imported a dog and bitch from the Avonia Kennel in Bristol. Since Miss Billet's death Miss Humby has carried on dog breeding and showing but uses the kennel name 'Humby's' and is strong in Avonia and Shiningcliff lines.

Among the current breeders and exhibitors who have been in the business for many years are:

Mr Fred Fraser of Ottawa, with his Ben Braggie Kennel. He has a long family association with the breed, for his grandfather, Daniel Fraser, bred them in Scotland before going to Canada, and his father Harry Fraser showed and bred them for 50 years. Mr Fraser imported Ch. Stoneygap Sugar Candy of Manraff and Ch. Stoneygap Bobbin of Gillobar, both from Mrs Barr.

Mrs J. H. Daniel-Jenkins (of the Rouge, 1947) imported Ch. Shiningcliff Sprig from Mrs Finch, winner of Best in Show and Groups. She has bred and made several U.S. and Canadian champions.

Mr and Mrs J. Neill Malcolm (Malcolms, 1948) are not very active in showing at present but they are still breeding. Mr Malcolm is a grandson of Colonel Malcolm of Poltalloch.

Mr and Mrs Albert A. Kaye (Dreamland, 1948) imported a number of young dogs from England, mostly puppies.

Mr and Mrs T. S. Adams (Roseneath, 1949), bred Amer. and Canad. Ch. Roseneath White Knight, winner of several Best in Shows and Groups. They imported Canad. Ch. Cruben Rhoda and Canad. Ch. Shiningcliff Sunflower. They are breeders of numerous U.S. Champions.

Mrs Sally Hudson of Vancouver imported from Mrs Beer Amer. Canad. Ch. Whitebriar Journeyman, who was winner of four Best in Show All Breeds, and three Best in Show All Terriers. He was the top winning West Highland in U.S. in 1963, being shown 26 times there and never defeated in the breed. During his U.S. show career Journeyman was in the temporary ownership of Mrs Barbara Sayers.

Amer. and Canad. Ch. Highland Ursa Major, bred by Miss Rosamond Billet and now owned by Mr Perry Chadwick, U.S., became the first West Highland to win the West Highland White Terrier Club of America Speciality Show and, as a stud dog, has made a very great contribution to the breed on the North American continent.

The West Highland White Terrier Club of Canada was
formed in 1951 and has held a Speciality Show every year
since. There are, currently, between 50 and 60 members. Some
of the most active breeders and exhibitors are:

Mr and Mrs T. S. Adams, Roseneath Kennels, Ontario.
Mr and Mrs Victor Blochin, Bencruachan Kennels, Ontario.
Mrs J. A. Bradley, Westlea Kennels, Alberta.
Mr and Mrs Eric Cox, Ervi Kennels, British Columbia.
Mrs J. H. Daniel-Jenkins, Kennels of the Rouge, Ontario.
Mr and Mrs H. N. Flannagan, Manderley Kennels, Ontario.
Mr and Mrs Albert A. Kaye, Dreamland Kennels, Ontario.
Mrs J. Neil Malcolm, Malcolms Kennels, Ontario.
Mr and Mrs R. S. McNicoll, Lochanside Kennels, Quebec.
Mr Fred Fraser, Ben Braggie Kennels, Ontario.
Mrs N. Freemantle, Remasaia Kennels, British Columbia.
Mrs S. J. Navin, Shipmates Kennels, British Columbia.
Mr and Mrs Ed. Payne, Dina-Ken Kennels, Nova Scotia.
Mr and Mrs Walter Stewart, Whinbrae Kennels, British
    Columbia.
Miss Edith Humby, Humby's Kennels, British Columbia.
Mr and Mrs James Scott, Macmoor Kennels, Ontario.
Col. D. and Miss Helen Seabrook, Stowe Kennels, Ontario.
Mrs Sally Hudson, Sallydean Kennels, British Columbia.

The most important All-breed Shows are held in Toronto,
Ottawa, with two shows, British Columbia with three shows,
Montreal, Quebec, one show. Circuit Shows are in the Mari-
time Provinces, Saskatchewan, Alberta, Port Arthur and
Winnipeg, Manitoba.

Two All-terrier shows are held in British Columbia, and two
in Ontario.

There are also a great many smaller shows held throughout
this vast country.

From the above it will be seen that the main centres of the
West Highland White Terrier population and Shows are
British Columbia and Ontario, but as they are separated by
more than 3,000 miles it is very rare for these exhibitors and
dogs to meet in competition.

The import regulations are very similar to those of the United States of America.

Australia

On 22nd September 1963 the first West Highland White Terrier Club in Australia was formed, with headquarters in Sydney. After nearly three years of existence, it boasts a membership extending from New South Wales to Queensland, Victoria, South Australia and to New Zealand. The first show was held on 15th November 1964, and for this occasion a beautiful trophy was donated by the West Highland White Terrier Club of Illinois, U.S.A., for Best in Show. The judge was Mr R. Burnell of Sydney, who awarded the top honour to English Ch. Busybody of Branston, with another importation, Wolvey Puritan, the C.C. winning dog.

Mr F. Luland of Sydney judged the second show in April 1965, and a perpetual trophy was donated by the Club President, Mrs E. Kohen. Best in Show again went to Busybody, the C.C. winning dog being her son Langsyne Philibeg by Baxter of Branston. At this show badges given by the 'of England' Club were awarded to class winners, proof indeed that the older clubs in England and America were extending a welcoming hand to the junior member of the clan.

The breed has been known in Australia for many years, even as far back as the beginning of the century, and has enjoyed considerable popularity before the Second World War and during the 1940s, but little was done to improve the breed for many years. There was some interchange of stock with New Zealand, but it was not until about 1960 that the breed began to be noticed at the shows. An analysis of entries for the Sydney Royal Easter Show gives an indication of the increasing popularity of Westies in recent years: 1961 (4), 1962 (3), 1963 (7), 1964 (15), 1965 (21).

Other statistics of interest are that in New South Wales in 1964, 15 litters were registered, 12 champions were made, and there were 5 exports, all to New Zealand.

It is reasonable to predict that the entries will increase for several years to come, gaining impetus through the medium of

a very progressive specialist club, and by the undisputed fact
that more effort has been spent on this breed than on any other
in the terrier group in New South Wales for some time.

In recent years some quality stock has been imported from
England to New South Wales. Mr Peter Brown of Goulburn
chose Pollyann of Patterscourt, Wolvey Provest, and two
Famecheck bitches, Nimble and Delibes, to augment his
'Peteraffles' Kennel. Mrs McEachern of Wagga, owning the
'Hielan' dogs, imported Wolvey Puritan. Then, in quick
succession, Famecheck Serenade, Baxter of Branston and the
English Ch. Busybody of Branston joined Miss B. Faulk's
'Langsyne' kennel.

Mr Phil Cunningham, in South Australia, has founded his
strain of 'Pilelo' Westies on a strong team of English dogs
and bitches, which include English Ch. Buttons of Helmsley,
Famecheck Lucrative and Stonygap Freddie, all well known at
English shows.

The impact of this imported blood is beginning to be felt,
resulting in increased success at the shows, and a demand by
show people for quality stock. The majority of breeders are
anxious to maintain quality, which policy, it is hoped, will
eventually give Australian West Highland White Terriers
world recognition.

Now that air travel is so commonplace in this vast country
the prospect of sending a bitch by air anything between one
and three thousand miles will not deter them from choosing
and using the most desirable stud dog.

In Australia although they are very thankful for their
glorious sunshine, they admit that it is a handicap to those
who have to cope with white dogs. Importations from England
are never again quite as white as when they arrived in that
sundrenched land. This is applicable to any white or white-
marked dog and the creamy colour that soon appears need not
necessarily be a breed fault. This is perhaps a point that overseas judges, and particularly those from England, should bear
in mind.

The Regulations for the Importation of Dogs into Australia
are very strict but quite simple.

Dogs imported from any other country except New Zealand must undergo a quarantine period of six months in England before being sent out by sea. Air travel will be permitted only on a non-stop flight between England and Australia, which at present is not feasible. Dogs born and bred in England obviously do not have to undergo the six months period.

On arrival in Australia, dogs are detained in quarantine for a period of 120 days. If, however, the Chief Quarantine Officer is satisfied that the dogs have not been in contact with any other dog at intermediate ports, the quarantine period may be reduced to 60 days. The present cost of quarantine for dogs over three months old is 3s. a day. Exporters are strongly advised to ship their dogs on vessels sailing direct to Australia, as if a dog is taken on board at any port outside Great Britain the full 120 days quarantine period will automatically apply.

Dogs exported from Great Britain may be shipped only at London, Southampton, Liverpool, Hull, Cardiff, Glasgow, Newport, Immingham, Birkenhead, Bristol, Avonmouth, Swansea, or Newcastle and may be landed in Australia at the following ports only: Fremantle, Port Adelaide, Melbourne, Sydney, Brisbane and Hobart.

All dogs travel on ship as 'deck cargo' and it is essential that the travelling kennel provided should be of adequate size for the six weeks' journey.

The following documents must accompany the dogs:
1. The Kennel Club Export Pedigree.
2. A statutory declaration by the owner stating:
    (1) that the dog has been in Great Britain during the whole of the period of six months preceding the date of shipment;
    (2) that during that period it has been free from disease, and
    (3) that it has not been in contact with any animal suffering from disease during that period.

This declaration must be made on form (E.D.I.) obtainable from the Ministry of Agriculture, Fisheries and Food, Livestock Export Division, Hook Rise South,

Tolworth, Surbiton, Surrey (Telephone Derwent 6611), *and must* be declared before a Magistrate or Commissioner for Oaths not earlier than a week before shipment.

The following are the diseases referred to above within the meaning of the Commonwealth of Australia Regulations:

Actinomycosis, anthrax, aujesky's disease, babesiosis, encephalitis, leptospirosis, mange, multiceps, multiceps infestation, piroplasmosis, rabies, rickettsiasis, stickfast flea, surra, tick infestation, trichinosis, trypanosomiasis, and tuberculosis.

3. A certificate from an approved veterinary surgeon at the port of shipment stating that the dog is free from disease and that, after due inquiry, he has no reason to doubt the truth of the owner's declaration. The names and addresses of these veterinary surgeons can be obtained from the Ministry.

4. A certificate on Part 2 of form (E.D.I.) from a veterinary surgeon who *must* be a Local Veterinary Inspector of the Ministry of Agriculture, Fisheries and Food stating that the dog has been subjected to a blood test for leptospirosis with negative results, within fourteen days of shipment. In the event of a vaccinated dog giving a positive reaction to the test for leptospirosis it may be re-tested four weeks later, and if neither test gives a higher titre than 1 : 100 the dog would be accepted for importation. The blood sample which should be at least 1 cc should be sent to the Ministry's Veterinary Laboratory at New Haw, Weybridge, Surrey.

Distemper and hepatitis are the only major diseases that affect dogs in Australia and both are very effectively controlled by immunisation.

The paralysis tick (Ixodes Holocyclus) is a menace along the Eastern coastline, being found in patches from North Queensland to Southern Tasmania, and, in some parts, extends inland. Various sprays and washes give some relief, even though temporary.

New Zealand

We are indebted to Mrs Harr, the secretary of the New Zealand Kennel Club, for the following information.

The history of dog showing in New Zealand goes back to my knowledge to around about 1886, and no doubt there were earlier Shows than this. In 1886 dog showing was conducted on an inter-provincial basis, and about this time the now New Zealand Kennel Club was first formed in Christchurch and in the early 1900s was transferred to Wellington.

One of the oldest present-day clubs is the Canterbury Kennel Club, formerly known as the Christchurch Dog Club, the Canterbury Club being formed in 1905 in Christchurch and holding its first Show in Hagley Park during the 1906 Exhibition year. This Club has now been operating for 59 years.

Until three years ago dog showing was operated on a four-group basis but some shows now operate on a six-group basis, as is done in Australia.

Today there are approximately 38 dog clubs throughout New Zealand, and once every year every club is invited to send delegates to the New Zealand Kennel Club Conference, and from these delegates the nucleus of the New Zealand Kennel Club Executive is elected as the Governing body for the dog fanciers of New Zealand. The rules and regulations for the registration of pure-bred dogs and for the conduct of shows are decided here, and permission obtained for the selection of judges to adjudicate at shows applied for by all dog clubs throughout New Zealand. This organisation has the distinction of being one of the few clubs affiliated to the Kennel Club of England.

Like every other country New Zealand has its problems for the dog fancier who wishes to import stock from overseas to improve his or her particular breed.

On the matter of quarantine regulations with regard to importing from other countries, to import from England does not require any imposition other than that, before the dog is landed in this country, it requires only a clearance from the Agricultural Department. I would like to point out here that up to four years ago there was a restriction which entailed isolating a dog for a period of sixty days, and it was not allowed to be shown before that period expired. This applied only to dogs imported from England. Today, however, they can be shown immediately on being landed.

With regard to imports from America and Europe this entails having a dog quarantined in England for a period of at least six months, and one brought direct from America to New Zealand, though frowned on by the Authorities, would, like other livestock, be placed on Soames Island, Wellington, for anything up to six or twelve months. This could also happen to a dog flown from England if the aeroplane landed en route at any place where rabies are considered to exist.

Another reason for quarantine would, of course, be with any dog from a declared tick area in Australia, and this could be the only reason for the declaration of quarantine in New Zealand.

It is possible to have dogs sent by air both from Australia and England, though, as I have mentioned previously, to do this from England is quite unsatisfactory owing to the quarantine regulations that operate if the plane lands en route.

The prevalent diseases with dogs in New Zealand seem to be principally distemper and hepatitis; things such as hardpad distemper have occurred only in one or two isolated cases.

Hydatids (type of tapeworm peculiar to New Zealand) are the greatest worry of the dog fancier at present; though not prevalent in show dogs, the fact that dogs have, in some areas, to be dosed three or four times a year causes a lot of worry. In the main cities dosing is once a year and is done on a house-to-house basis, other areas use a dosing strip!

According to Peggy Skey, of New Zealand, the first West Highland White Terriers imported into that country appear to have been by a Mr Hewitt, a chemist of Christchurch, in 1925–30. Later he sold some stock to Mr G. McKay of Somerfield, Christchurch. In 1931 Mr and Mrs Voice purchased a dog puppy from Mr McKay and in 1932 a bitch puppy from Mr Baylis of Auckland. In 1934 they also imported a dog and bitch from Mrs McCracken of Sydney, Australia.

Among other early breeders were Mr John Macdonald of Timaru, Mr Williams of Hawks Bay, Mr T. O'Connor of

Dunedin, and in 1935 Mr A. B. Cook of Christchurch started his well-known Avalon Kennels.

Sweden

In 1912 the first West Highland White Terrier was imported from Scotland—a bitch called Bubbles—and was quickly followed by a dog and another bitch, Bubbly under the Steeple, but it appears that no breeding was done.

In 1930 breeding was started by Mrs Marna Boothy-Philip who imported the bitch Clint Chieftainess and, a year later, made the first homebred champions with Dinomin Drabant and Dinomin Surprise.

This started interest in the breed, and the next breeder was Miss Marta Olsson, quickly followed by Mrs Lalla Hoglund and Mrs Elin Svensson, the latter with the prefix 'av Mariedal'. Both founded their kennels on the Dinomin blood lines and each imported stud dogs: Mrs Hoglund, Brean Kivvan, and Mrs Svensson, Wolvey Planter. It was the blood lines from these dogs, and Mrs Boothy-Philip's earlier import, Fearless Favourite, that were the stud force during the time of the Second World War. In about 1943 the breed appears to have slumped and Mrs Svensson was virtually alone.

In about 1950, West Highland White Terriers started to pick up when Mr Eric Werner imported several dogs, including Tachrian Petrarch and the bitch Thimble of Deanscourt, and both soon became champions. Also, Mrs Svensson imported Wolvey Pharoah, and Miss Olsson purchased Craig of Kendrum which became an international champion, and sired several champions, including the bitch Ch. Dox Fia, which became the foundation of Mrs Barbro Eklund's Mac Mahon Kennels. Mated to Wolvey Pharoah's son, Ch. Macky av Mariedal produced International Ch. MacMahons Vicke Vire, who has sired thirteen champions.

At about this same time, Mrs Hervor Hornfelt started her 'Coras' Kennel and imported Wolvey Pipe, who produced Ch. Coras Pamela. Other imports include Wolvey Party Suit and Wolvey Pierina.

During the past few years Mrs Barbro Eklund has imported

many dogs among whom have been Lasara Lennie and Lasara
Lutine, both becoming champions, Sollershot Stepson and Joy
of Wynsolot.

Recently, several new exhibitors have come to the front in
the breed, among them Miss Britta Roos with Swedish Ch.
Bushey of Branston, Miss Bargitta Reyman with Sollershot So
Sweet, and The Countess Hamilton with Benefactor of
Branston and Sollershot Sparkle.

The West Highland White Terrier Club of Sweden was
founded in 1965.

The regulations for the importation of dogs into Sweden
require that the importer shall obtain a licence from the
Swedish Ministry of Agriculture and that the dog has a blood
test for leptospirae taken within ten days of the date of de-
parture. The blood sample is normally taken by the exporter's
veterinary surgeon and must be sent for test to the
Ministry of Agriculture research laboratories at Weybridge,
Surrey, who, if the test is satisfactory, will issue a negative
certificate. This certificate must be certified by the Livestock
Division of the Ministry of Agriculture.

The normal Health Certificate and Kennel Club Export
Pedigree are also required.

The Nordic Countries, with Sweden leading the way, are
showing exceptional interest in the breed. Mrs Birgitta
Hasselgren, whose Nordic Ch. Tweed Tartan Maid has
become the top leading champion in Sweden, is Secretary of
the Swedish West Highland White Terrier Club and one
among so many other enthusiastic breeders of Westies in that
lovely country.

Western Germany

In the past few years several West Highland White Terriers
have been exported to West Germany and I have been informed
that their popularity increases every year. One of the leading
exhibitors and breeders is Mr O. Flerlage of Osnabrook.

The import regulations require only the Health Certificate
and Kennel Club Export Pedigree. It is, however, imperative
that any dog sent to Germany *must* have a full complement of

42 teeth, as without this number a dog is debarred from exhibition.

Japan
The Japanese have been showing great interest in West Highlands and several dogs have been imported from Britain and America, but it is regretted that very little information is available about breeding, exhibiting or import regulations.

Southern Africa
Mrs E. Wride of Lusaka, Zambia, keeps the flag flying for the breed in the African continent, classes being scheduled at shows in Zambia, Southern Rhodesia and South Africa.

Rhodesia
Rhodesia has no West Highland club as yet, but interest in the breed seems definitely on the increase as fresh good imports arrive to make their presence felt in the showring. Mrs P. Campbell of the 'Inverleith' prefix in Bulawayo is hoping with recent imports to build up a strong team and it is hoped that before too long the breed will receive the acknowledgement it deserves as one of the most distinctive of all the terriers.

Ritter

American Ch. Purston Pinmoney Pedlar, 1972

Boz

Ch. Gaywyn Bradey of Branston, 1972

Ch. Carillyon Cadence, 1975

Anne Roslin-Williams

Ch. Glenalwyne Sonny Boy, 1975

13

Some Ailments and Treatment

EVERY owner of a dog, whether it be one or a dozen, should know where to find a good veterinary surgeon, and have his address and telephone number in the address book. Often prompt professional advice and attention, whether the emergency is caused by illness or perhaps a road accident, is all that can save a dog's life. Most dogs may never need his services except when they are inoculated in puppyhood. Today, a large variety of modern drugs and antibiotics can save dogs from suffering, and indeed, from what would have been certain death years ago. Inoculations against distemper and hardpad have reduced the risk of losing a dog from either of these two infectious diseases to a very low level.

The general public tend to blame every kind of illness suffered by a pedigree dog to the fact that it is what they call 'highly bred'. Inbreeding, or being 'highly bred', has more often than not little if anything to do with it. Dogs, like people, are mainly healthy, but they are just as prone to upsets of various kinds for no apparent reason as that their owners are to attacks of flu or gastritis. Any owner who really cares for his dog will soon notice if it is off its food, in the same way that a fond mother notices at once if Johnny doesn't relish his porridge. The dog may have merely an upset stomach which a condition powder will soon put right, but the wise owner will be on the alert for more serious developments. It is fairly easy to keep close watch on a pet dog that is a little off colour and to see whether it regains its appetite later in the day and is ready for its usual exercise. With a large kennel of perhaps thirty or forty dogs it is a different matter and needs a practised eye to spot promptly the dog that is not in its usual sparkling form.

H

For this reason, if for no other, it is advisable that the owner or some other responsible person should make a routine check early in the day. The best time of all is first thing in the morning when the kennel doors are opened. With the urge to be up and doing, that is the natural way of a healthy Westie, any dog that emerges from its kennel in a sluggish manner with its tail down calls for a second look. My experience is that as their kennel doors are opened they hurtle out like jet-propelled missiles even on the coldest mornings. If one does appear to be a bit off form, watch how it behaves for five minutes or so. The trouble may be nothing more than a cyst between the toes or an inflamed ear causing discomfort, constipation, or indigestion. Any of these treated with some simple but appropriate remedy may quickly be relieved. Should the dog, however, be shivery and hump-backed, take its temperature immediately. A clinical thermometer is an absolutely vital piece of equipment and there should always be a spare one in the medicine chest to replace a broken one. The temperature is one of the surest guides to judging the seriousness of your dog's indisposition. The thermometer should be lightly greased with Vaseline and gently inserted about an inch into the rectum, and left for at least one minute.

If the bowels are easily moved and the excreta is normal it is unlikely that the stomach is out of order. But should there be any sign of diarrhoea, take careful note of how frequently the bowels are moved and, if the diarrhoea is excessive, give a mixture of bismuth and chalk, isolate the dog, and keep it warm and comfortable. If it fails to react to this simple treatment do not delay in getting the veterinary surgeon, for it may easily be the beginning of something more serious. If people would learn to keep their eyes open and really 'see' a dog when they look at it, a lot of trouble would be saved, for the dogs and everyone concerned. Never defer, because you are busy, giving attention to an ailing dog. With long-haired dogs, if the hair is not regularly kept short round the anus and parts immediately surrounding it, the long hair becomes soiled and if not attended to the dog quickly gets into an unpleasant state and becomes miserable. Train yourself, or anyone that has the care of the dog or dogs, to see this sort of thing automatically at a glance and to deal with it without delay.

The normal temperature of a dog is about 101½°F, but, like humans, it can vary slightly. So, if on taking a temperature the first time and the thermometer reads 102 degrees, don't conclude too hastily that the dog is ill but watch it closely to see whether it is off its food, whether it vomits or not, and what its bowel action is like. If the temperature continues to rise and continues upwards over 102½ degrees, then it is time to call for professional advice. Having placed the dog in some warm place, completely isolated from all other dogs, leave it to rest quietly. Do not try to force a dog running a high temperature to eat. A bowl of fresh cold water to allay its thirst is all that is necessary at first, and then later in the day offer it a dish of warm milk sweetened with honey. Pure honey is always beneficial for its food value and healing properties.

If you keep a number of dogs and have litters of small puppies, never go straight from any dog that is ailing to the young puppies, or anything else if it can be avoided, without first taking the precaution of washing your hands, changing your shoes and changing anything like an overall or top coat that may have come in contact with a sick dog that you have been attending to. It is better to be ultra cautious about spreading any infection in the beginning. In the same way, extra care about disinfecting a kennel in which a sick dog has been housed is of great importance if germs are to be prevented from spreading. Scrub it out using either strong soda water or water with strong disinfectant. Get right into the corners and move everything movable. In the fairly rare event of a virulent infection occurring in kennels, the safest way to sterilise sleeping boxes, etc., if they are too valuable to be burnt, is to use a blow-lamp. Fortunately, the degree of immunity now enjoyed, through the benefits of inoculation, from serious outbreaks of distemper, etc., make the more drastic methods very rarely necessary.

If you are not sure of your diagnosis be sure to get professional advice before it is too late.

Abscess. This is most painful, the dog being reluctant to move about more than is absolutely necessary. It should be treated by poulticing frequently with Kaolin which draws it to a head, when it should burst. If it does not burst of its own accord when it is ripe it can be opened with a well-sterilised sharp pointed knife. The wound should then be bathed several times a day with warm salt and water and kept open until it is quite clean.

Anal Glands. These are troublesome in older dogs if neglected. The usual sign that the glands need emptying is evidenced by a dog dragging its hindquarters along the ground. Any intense irritation round the hindquarters of a dog should give rise to suspicion of anal gland trouble. It is often mistaken for worms. The treatment is quite simple. Place the dog on the table, grasping the tail in the left hand. Take a large piece of cotton-wool in the right hand and apply pressure, starting from a little more than an inch below the anus and gradually closing the finger and thumb as you press upwards. It is often possible to feel a little hard lump on either side. With firm pressure the secretion can be ejected into the cotton-wool. If left unattended this condition can cause an abscess.

Appetite. If the adult dog shows a craving for dirt and evil-smelling muck it is almost certainly a sign of lack of mineral salts in its diet. The diet should be supplemented with calcium lactate and seaweed, from which they appear to derive much benefit.

Constipation. If seen in the early stages of the first day or two it is usually cleared by adding raw, roughly grated carrots and finely chopped raw cabbage to the dog's food and giving a dessertspoonful of liquid paraffin before each meal. In the event of the bowels not being moved easily after a reasonable lapse of time further investigation should be undertaken by a veterinary surgeon to find out if a foreign body is obstructing the intestines.

Diarrhoea. This most often occurs in very young puppies
and can quickly cause death if not given prompt attention. It
may be caused by a germ, especially if the puppies are only a
few days old. At this age only an antibiotic injection given
promptly is likely to save them. Later, the trouble is more
likely to be caused by a chill or sleeping on a wet bed or being
fed with unsuitable food that is over-rich or that has become
stale or sour. The dog should be given a diet of white of an
egg, arrowroot gruel and B.P. lime water in equal quantities.
In more severe cases a dose of three drops of chlorodyne in a
little water given three times a day is very helpful. As the condition inproves, keep to a rather light diet free from greasiness
for a few days.

If severe in adults it may herald the beginning of a virus
disease. If the temperature is high, say 103 degrees, promp
professional attention is required. It is especially important to
see that hygienic conditions are observed.

Ear Canker. There are several forms of ear trouble, all often
loosely referred to as canker. The most common is usually
caused by a microscopic insect that betrays its appearance by a
rather sticky, dirty dark discharge. If left unattended the discharge may become very hard, when it is necessary to soften it
with warm olive oil before it is possible to clean the ear completely without hurting the ear. Once the discharge is softened,
with cotton-wool round an orange stick, gently lift out all the
filth. When the ear is thoroughly cleansed and wiped dry with
cotton-wool apply one of the proprietary creams or other
products available. A liquid or a cream emollient is better than
anything in powder form, which has a tendency to clog the
ear. Whatever form the irritation takes it must have daily
attention if the condition is to be cleared up. If there is no
apparent improvement after a week or so it is advisable to
change to some other dressing. The condition, if not cured, can
cause acute discomfort.

Eclampsia. This occurs usually when a bitch is nursing a
litter, but it can happen prior to whelping. It is caused by the

excessive drain of calcium from the system. The symptoms are shivering, and rapid panting, and the bitch will stagger around and sometimes collapse completely. There must be no delay in getting veterinary assistance. If treated promptly she will usually return to normal in an hour or so. Any delay in treatment will almost certainly prove fatal within a few hours.

Eczema. Rarely found among West Highlands, any slight irritation of the skin will, if neglected, eventually develop into eczema. First steps should be to purify the blood and tone up the condition generally by giving a teaspoonful of seaweed powder mixed into the main meal of the day. Dogs usually have no dislike of the seaweed powder and take their food quite readily when it is well mixed in. They may drink a little more water until they become accustomed to taking the seaweed powder, which can be continued indefinitely because it is beneficial to the diet at all times. Chopped raw carrots and cabbage should also be mixed in the food.

Wash the dog with a good antiseptic dog shampoo. See that the bedding is kept scrupulously clean, and if blankets are used they must be changed daily if possible. Any bedding such as wood-wool, straw or hay which might irritate the skin should be avoided.

Gastritis. This is an inflammation of the stomach, usually caused by eating sour or unsuitable food. The dog should be kept on a light diet of milk and barley-water and honey until the condition subsides. It will often show a craving for water and, having taken a large amount, will promptly vomit it up again. Remove the drinking bowl of water so that the only liquid available for the time being is the milk and barley-water. Keep the dog quiet and very warm and if the vomiting is severe and sustained get further advice from your veterinary adviser.

Metritis. This usually occurs within a few days of whelping and is often caused by the retention of one or more afterbirth, which causes inflammation of the uterus. The signs are vomiting, restlessness and reluctance to take food. The temperature will rise quickly and professional advice should be called for. Modern antibiotics when correctly and promptly used usually effect a speedy cure.

Worms. The two types most frequently found in the U.K. are round worms and tape worms. Round worms are the ones that generally have to be dealt with. If a bitch with puppies has not been wormed before breeding or shortly after being mated, the puppies will almost certainly get them. All puppies, irrespective of whether they appear to have worms or not, should be dosed at the latest by six weeks, and again at eight weeks to make sure that they are completely cleared. Present-day medicines are safe and easy to administer and do not upset the puppies. Once puppies have been properly wormed they do not often easily become infested again if kept under hygienic conditions. Puppies thrive much more after they have been cleared of worms. There is no harm in worming a dog once in six months if it is suspected that it has become re-infested.

Tape worms are less frequently found, and very rarely in puppies. Dogs kept clean and free of fleas, which are the host of the intermediate stage of the tape worm, are unlikely to become infected. Successful destruction of the tape worm can be difficult to achieve as the head is embedded in the bowel and only segments are expelled. Until the whole of the tape worm is expelled the growth will be repeated. Many good proprietary medicines are on the market for the removal of worms but for tape worms a more drastic vermifuge is required if success is to be assured, and it is often best to have veterinary supervision so that no harm may be done.

So that no other dogs may become infected, always burn, at once, expelled worms or any excreta that may contain worms.

Inoculations. A great deal of anxiety about contagious disease has in the last decade been removed from all dog breeders. The very efficient vaccines now commonly in use have given all vaccinated dogs a greater expectation of life. The perils of taking valuable dogs to shows and, in particular, large indoor winter shows has been removed by the use of the various vaccines available. Every dog breeder when selling a puppy that has not already been immunised against hardpad and distemper should obtain a promise from the buyer that the puppy will be kept away from any chance of becoming infected by any other dogs until such time as it is old enough to be immunised, which is usually accepted as no younger than twelve weeks old. It is possible to inoculate at an earlier age than twelve weeks, but the dose needs to be repeated to ensure satisfactory immunity.

It is now possible to have dogs inoculated against the five following diseases: *Distemper and hardpad*, *leptospira canicola infection* (bacteria which attack the kidneys), *leptospica icterohaemorrhacaciae infection* (related to leptospira canicola but causing jaundice), an infection usually transmitted by rats, *contagious virus hepatitis* (Rubarth's Disease), a virus infection that attacks the liver.

Every kennel should have a medicine cupboard. Different lotions, powders and pills will be collected as the need arises but a few essentials are in almost daily use. They are cottonwool, Dettol, T.C.P., olive oil, liquid paraffin, worm tablets, Pulvex, and, of course, a thermometer or, better still, two. If pills or medicines are prescribed, always see that the directions and purpose for which they are intended are clearly written on the bottle or box.

WORLD BREED CLUBS

West Highland White Terrier Club. Formed 1905.
Secretary: Mrs E. M. Campbell, Meadowfield, Cluney Place,
Edinburgh 10. *Tel.:* 031-447 4906.

West Highland White Terrier Club of England. Formed 1905.
Secretary: Mrs H. Davies, Clynebury Lodge, Great North Road,
Chesterton, near Peterborough, Northamptonshire. *Tel.:*
Castor 311.

West Highland White Terrier Club of Ireland.
Secretary: Mrs E. Morrow, 3 Taney Road, Dundrum, Dublin 14,
Eire.

West Highland White Terrier Club of Northern Ireland. **Formed**
1959.
Secretary: Mr I. W. Bradley, The Bungalow, Carrowdore,
Gransha, Bangor, Co. Down, N. Ireland. *Tel.:* Bangor 60005.

The West Highland White Terrier Club of America. Formed 1909.
Secretary: Mrs J. W. Williams, Jr, 3524 Kirkby Lane, Jefferson
Town, Ky 40299, U.S.A.

West Highland White Terrier Club of Washington. Formed 1951.
Secretary: Louise Simon, 3011 Maple Drive, Fairfax, Va 20030,
U.S.A.

West Highland White Terrier Club of California.
Secretary: Helen Love, 373 Fowling, Playa del Rey, California
90291, U.S.A.

West Highland White Terrier Club of Indiana.
Secretary: Mrs John Niermeyer, 10679 Highland Drive, Carmel,
Indiana, U.S.A.

West Highland White Terrier Club of New York.
Secretary: Mrs Mary Pross, 185–32–80th Road, Jamaica Estates, New York 11432, U.S.A.

West Highland White Terrier Club of New England.
Secretary: Mr Chris Swingle, 218 Pine Acres, Canton, Conn. 06019, U.S.A.

West Highland White Terrier Club of Chicago.
Secretary: Mrs Peggy Hass, RT2 Box 164, Plainfield, Illinois 60544, U.S.A.

West Highland White Terrier Club of Northern California.
Secretary: Mrs Pat Winans, 8611 Carlisle Avenue, Sacramento, California 95828, U.S.A.

West Highland White Terrier Club of Trinity Valley.
Secretary: Bessie Land, 78–30 Claremont Drive, Dallas, Texas 75228, U.S.A.

West Highland White Terrier Club of Northern Ohio.
Secretary: Mrs Nina Moses, 29159 Chardon Road, Wickliffe, Ohio 44092, U.S.A.

West Highland White Terrier Club of Southern Texas.
Secretary: Mrs Judy Clark, 13502 Robbins, Cypress, Texas 77429, U.S.A.

West Highland White Terrier Club of Canada. Formed 1951.
***Secretary:* Mr H. N. Flanagan, Manderley Kennels, R.R. I., Brooklin, Ontario.**

West Highland White Terrier Club of Australia. Formed 1963.
Secretary: Mrs J. Peck, 20 Lawson Road, Milpo Ingleburn, 2174 New South Wales, Australia.

West Highland White Terrier Club of Sweden. Formed 1965.
Secretary: Miss Suzanne Birberg, Tegner Garten 17, 11140 Stockholm, Sweden.

WEST HIGHLAND WHITE TERRIER CHAMPIONS 1947 to 1975

Name	Sex	Sire	Dam	Owner	Breeder	Born
1947						
Betty of Whitehills	B	Garvie O' The Hills	Say Nought	Mrs V. Swan	Mrs F. Barr	27-2-44
Freshney Fiametta	B	Melbourne Mathias	Freshney Felicia	Miss E. E. Wade	Mrs M. McKinney	10-12-43
Shiningcliff Simon	D	Ch. Leal Flurry	Walney Thistle	Mrs J. Finch	Mrs J. Finch	10-5-45
Timosshenko of the Roe	D	Irish Champ. Tam O' Shanter of the Roe	Whisper of the Roe	The Hon. Torfrida Tollo	Mrs E. M. Garnett	23-3-45
1948						
Baffle of Branston	B	Freshney Frinton	Baroness of Branston	Mrs D. M. Dennis	Mrs D. M. Dennis	13-9-46
Cruben Crystal	B	Freshney Andy	Cruben Miss Seymour	Dr & Mrs A. Russel	Dr & Mrs A. Russel	9-3-46
Deirdre of Kendrum	B	Roddy of Whitehills	Gyl of Kendrum	The Hon. T. H. Rollo	The Hon. T. H. Rollo	23-8-46
Hookwood Mentor	D	Furzefield Piper	Bonchurch Bunty	Miss E. E. Wade	Mr A. Brown	14-5-47
Macairns Jemima	B	Ch. Leal Sterling	Macairns Jeannie	Mr C. Drake	Mr C. Drake	1-8-43
Pygmalion of Patterscourt	D	Ch. Melbourne Mathias	Pola of Patterscourt	Mr W. Patterson	Mr W. Patterson	19-12-45
Wolvey Prospect	D	Ch. Wolvey Prefect	Wolvey Poise	Mrs C. Pacey	Mrs C. Pacey	14-10-44
1949						
Athos of Whitehills	D	Freshney Andy	Julie of Whitehills	Mrs V. M. Swam	Mrs V. M. Swam	18-12-45
Binnie of Branston	B	Freshney Andy	Belinda of Branston	Mrs D. M. Dennis	Mrs D. M. Dennis	28-8-45
Furzefield Pax	D	Furzefield Piper	Cassette of Eastfield	Mrs D. P. Allom	Mrs D. P. Allom	11-11-47
Heathcote Freshney Flare	B	Freshney Niall	Freshney Farel	Mrs N. Baxter	Mrs M. McKinney	3-4-47

Name	Sex	Sire	Dam	Owner	Breeder	Born
1949—contd. Lorne Jock	D	Freshney Andy	Fuff Ici	Messrs McEwan & McVicar	Messrs McEwan & McVicar	10-7-46
Macconachie Tiena Joy	B	Ch. Shiningcliff Simon	Macconachie Pearlie	Mr A. H. Salsbury	Mr A. H. Salsbury	27-10-47
Shiningcliff Storm	D	Leal Pax	Walney Thistle	Mr H. S. Hallas	Mrs J. Finch	13-11-46
Wolvey Penelope	B	Wolvey Parole	Wolvey Poise	Mrs C. Pacey	Mrs C. Pacey	5-11-45
Wolvey Prudence	B	Wolvey Premier	Wolvey Plume	Mrs C. Pacey	Mrs. C. Pacey	15-5-45
1950 Barrister of Branston	D	Ch. Hockwood Mentor	Bloom of Branston	Mrs D. M. Dennis	Mrs D. M. Dennis	1-12-48
Brisk of Branston	D	Ch. Hookwood Mentor	Bloom of Branston	Mrs J. G. Winant	Mrs D. M. Dennis	11-7-49
Furzefield Preference	B	Furzefield Piper	Casette of Eastfield	Miss E. E. Wade	Mrs D. P. Allom	28-5-49
Heathcolne Roamer	D	Am. Ch. Cruben Silver Birk	Heathcolne Peggy Walker	Mrs N. M. Baxter	Mrs N. M. Baxter	14-1-44
Isla of Kendrum	B	Furzefield Piper	Ch. Deirdre of Kendrum	The Hon. T. Rollo	The Hon. T. Rollo	8-5-49
Maree of Kendrum	B	Furzefield Piper	Ch. Deirdre of Kendrum	The Hon. T. Rollo	The Hon. T. Rollo	8-5-49
Shiningcliff Sprig	D	Ch. Shiningcliff Simon	Freshney Folly	Mrs J. Finch	Mrs J. Finch	3-8-47
1951 Cruben Dextor	D	Ch. Hookwood Mentor	Am. Ch. Cruben Melphis Chloe	Dr & Mrs Russel	Dr & Mrs Russel	17-1-50
Crystone Chatterer	B	Cruben Faerdele	Heathcolne Frolic	Mrs E. Anthony	Mrs E. Anthony	30-5-49
Chrystone Cherry	B	Ch. Heathcolne Roamer	Cryston Crystal	Mrs E. Anthony	Mrs E. Anthony	7-9-49

124

Furzefield Provost	D	Furzefield Piper	Calluna Nike	Mrs D. P. Allom	Miss A. A. Wright	30-10-48
Hookwood Sensation	D	Ch. Hookwood Mentor	Ch. Freshney Fiametta	Miss E. E. Wade	Miss E. E. Wade	11-2-49
Lynwood Branston Blue	B	Ch. Hookwood Mentor	Bloom of Branston	Mrs M. G. Ellis	Mrs D. M. Dennis	2-12-48
Mallaig Silver Empress	B	Cruben Silver Birk	Mallaig Pola Maid	Miss E. E. Wade	Mr E. Bagshaw	22-6-47
Mark of Old Trooper	D	Ch. Shiningcliff Simon	Dainty Dinkie	Mr E. Ward	Mr E. Ward	17-1-48
Shiningcliff Snowcloud	B	Ch. Shiningcliff Simon	Shiningcliff Snow White	Mrs J. Finch	Mrs J. Finch	15-3-47
Shiningcliff Sultan	D	Ch. Melbourne Mathias	Walney Thistle	Mrs J. Finch	Mrs J. Finch	21-11-48
Staplands Shepherd	D	Shiningcliff Shardy	Cestrian Kilry	Mr & Mrs H. T. Walsh	Mr & Mrs H. T. Walsh	27-2-49
1952 Brush of Branston	B	Int. Ch. Brisk of Branston	Binty of Branston	Mrs D. M. Dennis	Mrs D. M. Dennis	3-10-50
Cotsmoor Crunch	B	Hookwood Mentor	Cotsmoor Crisp	Mrs R. Capper	Mrs R. Capper	26-3-50
Furzefield Pilgrim	D	Furzefield Piper	Furzefield Purpose	Mrs D. P. Allom	Mrs D. P. Allom	27-1-51
Hasty Bits	D	Claregate Benjamin of Branston	Walfield Fleur	Mrs G. M. Barr	Mrs G. M. Barr	13-12-50
Heathcolne Gowan	B	Ch. Heathcolne Roamer	Heathcolne White Sprig	Mrs F. M. Brownridge	Mrs N. Baxter	16-6-48
Perchance of Patterscourt	B	Petronius of Patterscourt	Perrow of Patterscourt	Mrs R. M. Jones	Mr W. J. Patterson	9-5-48
Shiningcliff Dunthorne Damsel	B	Shiningcliff Shardy	Pathton of Patterscourt	Mrs J. Finch	Mrs G. Thorneycroft	18-2-49
Staplands Spitfire	D	Ch. Staplands Shepherd	Staplands Saint	Mr & Mrs H. T. Walsh	Mr & Mrs H. T. Walsh	9-7-50

Name	Sex	Sire	Dam	Owner	Breeder	Born
1952—contd. Wolvey Piquet	B	Wolvey Presto	Wolvey Patsy	Mrs C. Pacey	Mrs C. Pacey	9-8-50
Wolvey Poster	D	Ch. Wolvey Prospect	Wolvey Phrolic	Mrs C. Pacey	Mrs C. Pacey	27-3-50
1953 Calluna the Poacher	D	Calluna Bingo	Calluna Vermintrude	Mrs A. Beels	Mrs A. Beels	27-3-52
Cotsmoor Cream Puff	B	Ch. Barrister of Branston	Cotsmoor Crisp	Mrs R. K. Capper	Mrs R. K. Capper	20-8-51
Cruben Moray	D	Int. Ch. Cruben Dextor	Cruben Fancy	Dr & Mrs Russell	Dr & Mrs Russell	8-9-51
Hookwood Gardenia	B	Ch. Hookwood Mentor	Barassie Bright Beam	Mrs G. M. Barr	Mr H. Galt	25-1-50
Lynwood Blue Betty	B	Furzefield Piper	Ch. Lynwood Branston Blue	Mr & Mrs G. Ellis	Mr & Mrs G. Ellis	21-7-50
Lynwood Timothy	D	Furzefield Piper	Ch. Lynwood Branston Blue	Mr & Mrs G. Ellis	Mr & Mrs G. Ellis	28-1-52
Rosalan Rogue	D	Ch. Hookwood Sensation	Rosalan Regina	Miss E. E. Wade	Mrs D. A. Phillips	13-5-51
Shiningcliff Donark Decision	D	Ch. Shiningcliff Simon	Donark Determined	Mrs F. Finch	Mrs L. Dwyer	17-4-50
Shiningcliff Sugar Plum	B	Ch. Shiningcliff Simon	Thalia of Trenean	Mrs F. Finch	Mrs G. Frost	1-4-51
Wolvey Peach	B	Wolvey Presto	Wolvey Patsy	Mrs C. Pacey	Mrs C. Pacey	9-8-50
Wolvey Poppet	B	Wolvey Paramount	Wolvey Peach	Mrs C. Pacey	Mrs C. Pacey	24-12-51
1954 Bannock of Branston	D	Ch. Barrister of Branston	Binty of Branston	Mrs D. M. Dennis	Mrs D. M. Dennis	11-6-52
Biretta of Branston	B	Ch. Barrister of Branston	Ch. Babble of Branston	Mrs D. M. Dennis	Mrs D. M. Dennis	30-5-52
Cotsmoor Creambun	B	Ch. Barrister of Branston	Cotsmoor Crisp	Mrs R. Capper	Mrs R. Capper	30-8-51

	D/B	Sire	Dam	Breeder	Owner	Date
Eoghan of Kendrum	D	Ch. Barrister of Branston	Ch. Isla of Kendrum	Hon. T. Rollo	Hon. T. Rollo	3-7-52
Famecheck Lucky Charm	B	Ch. Shiningcliff Sultan	Famecheck Paddy Scalare	Miss F. M. C. Cook	Miss F. M. C. Cook	5-2-53
Laird of Lochalan	D	Ch. Rosalan Rogue	Susan of Northcliff	Mrs R. W. Scott	Mrs R. W. Scott	29-12-52
Mairi of Kendrum	B	Ch. Barrister of Branston	Ch. Isla of Kendrum	Miss J. Herbert	Hon. T. Rollo	21-1-51
Tulyar of Trenean	D	Int. Ch. Cruben Dextor	Heathcolne Thistle	Mrs W. Dodgson	Mrs W. Dodgson	2-7-52
Wolvey Pageboy	D	Wolvey Paramount	Ch. Wolvey Peach	Mrs C. Pacey	Mrs C. Pacey	24-12-51
1955 Brendale	B	Fruin of Kendrum	Dainty Brenda	Mrs H. M. Jeffrey	Mrs H. M. Jeffrey	18-11-53
Famecheck Viking	D	Ch. Calluna the Poacher	Famecheck Fluster	Miss F. M. C. Cook	Miss F. M. C. Cook	7-10-53
Lynwood Marcia	B	Ch. Wolvey Poster	Ch. Lynwood Branston Blue	Mr & Mrs G. Ellis	Mr & Mrs G. Ellis	10-2-53
Nice Fella of Wynsolot	D	Fan Mail of Wynsolot	Shiningcliff Starturn	Mrs E. A. Green	Mrs E. A. Green	24-5-53
Quakertown Quality	B	Ch. Calluna the Poacher	Calluna Miss Phoebe	Mr & Mrs H. Sansom	Mr & Mrs H. Sansom	13-2-54
Raventofts Fuchsia	B	Ch. Cruben Moray	Raventofts Periwinkle	Mrs N. Whitworth	Mrs N. Whitworth	10-1-53
Rowmore Brora of Kennishead	D	Int. Ch. Cruben Dextor	Cinda of Kennishead	Miss I. Maclean Cowie	Miss I. Maclean Cowie	10-6-52
Slitrig Solitaire	B	Ch. Furzefield Pilgrim	Slitrig Sequin	Mrs C. M. Kirby	Mrs C. M. Kirby	19-9-53
1956 Banda of Branston	B	Ch. Barrister of Branston	Binty of Branston	Mrs D. W. Dennis	Mrs D. W. Dennis	16-8-54
Bramhill Patricia	B	Calluna Big Wig	Bramhill Beatrix	Mrs J. H. Gee	Mrs J. H. Gee	9-11-53
Broomheather Fianna	B	Int. Ch. Cruben Moray	Broomheather Flora	Mrs E. Hay	Mrs E. Hay	21-8-54

Name	Sex	Sire	Dam	Owner	Breeder	Born
1956—contd. Famecheck Gay Crusader	D	Ch. Famecheck Happy Knight	Ch. Famecheck Lucky Charm	Miss F. M. C. Cook	Miss F. M. C. Cook	7-9-54
Famecheck Happy Knight	D	Ch. Calluna the Poacher	Famecheck Fluster	Miss F. M. C. Cook	Miss F. M. C. Cook	7-10-53
Slitrig Shandy	D	Ch. Barrister of Branston	Ch. Slitrig Solitaire	Mrs C. M. Kirby	Mrs C. M. Kirby	22-5-55
Wolvey Patricia	B	Wolvey Poster	Ch. Wolvey Peach	Mrs C. Pacey	Mrs C. Pacey	30-8-54
Wolvey Philippa	B	Ch. Wolvey Poster	Ch. Wolvey Peach	Mrs C. Pacey	Mrs C. Pacey	30-8-54
Wolvey Pied Piper	D	Furzefield Pilgrim	Wolvey Padella	Mrs C. Pacey	Mrs C. Pacey	14-4-55
1957 Banker of Branston	D	Ch. Barrister of Branston	Binty of Branston	Mrs D. M. Dennis	Mrs D. M. Dennis	8-5-56
Cruben Chilibeam	B	Ch. Calluna the Poacher	Cruben Cutie	Dr & Mrs M. Russell	Dr & Mrs M. Russell	16-8-54
Crystone Cressina	B	Calluna Big Wig	Crystone Charmong	Mrs E. Anthony	Mrs E. Anthony	12-12-55
Famecheck Ballet Dancer	B	Ch. Famecheck Viking	Famecheck Silver Dollar	Mrs G. Bingham	Miss Cook	26-12-55
Famecheck Comet	B	Ch. Famecheck Gay Crusader	Ch. Famecheck Lucky Mascot	Mr A. Berry	Miss F. M. C. Cook	20-7-56
Famecheck Lucky Mascot	B	Ch. Shiningcliff Sultan	Famecheck Paddy Scalare	Miss F. M. C. Cook	Miss F. M. C. Cook	5-2-53
Kirnbrae Symmetra Sailaway	D	Int. Ch. Cruben Moray	Denmohr Gay Girl	Miss J. Brown	Miss J. Brown	15-10-53
Mistymoor Andrea	B	Ch. Furzefield Pilgrim	Mistymoor Deirdre	Miss M. M. Batchelor	Miss M. M. Batchelor	2-11-54
Wolvey Pirate	D	Ch. Wolvey Pageboy	Wolvey Playmate	Mrs C. Pacey	Mrs C. Pacey	5-10-55

128

1958						
Brindle of Branston	B	Ch. Banker of Branston	Bono of Branston	Mrs D. M. Dennis	Mrs D. M. Dennis	22-4-57
Calluna the Laird	D	Ch. Laird of Lochalan	Calluna Sheenagh	Miss A. A. Wright	Miss A. A. Wright	1-12-56
Famecheck Gaiety Girl	B	Ch. Famecheck Gay Crusader	Ch. Famecheck Lucky Mascot	Miss F. M. C. Cook	Miss F. M. C. Cook	24-1-56
Famecheck Lucky Choice	B	Ch. Shiningcliff Sultan	Famecheck Paddy Scalare	Miss F. M. C. Cook	Miss F. M. C. Cook	24-9-53
Famecheck Jolly Warrior	D	Ch. Famecheck Happy Knight	Int. Ch. Famecheck Lucky Charm	Miss F. M. C. Cook	Miss F. M. C. Cook	25-2-55
Freshney Fray	B	Ch. Barrister of Branston	Freshney Flute	Mrs P. M. Welch	Mrs M. McKinney	25-8-54
Quakertown Questionaire	D	Ch. Eoghan of Kendrum	Quakertown Questionmark	Mrs K. Sansom	Mrs K. Sansom	8-8-55
Rivelin Rustle	B	Rivelin Renown	Cruben Margaret	Mrs M. W. Pearson	Mrs M. Tazzyman	16-12-55
Shiningcliff Sheela	B	Shiningcliff So-So	Miss Prim	Mrs F. Finch	Miss Holland	9-7-55
Sollershott Sun-up	D	Ch. Nice Fella of Wynsolot	Cotsmoor Crack O' Dawn	Mrs D. J. Kenney Taylor	Mrs D. J. Kenney Taylor	27-4-57
Stoneygap Commodore	D	Slitrig Skipper	Stoneygap Twig	Mrs G. M. Barr	Mrs G. M. Barr	23-5-57
Wolvey Piper's Son	D	Ch. Wolvey Pied Piper	Wolvey Pennywise	Mrs C. Pacey	Mrs C. Pacey	10-5-57
Wolvery Postmaster	D	Ch. Wolvey Poster	Wolvey Paulina	Mrs C. Pacey	Mrs C. Pacey	29-5-56
1959 Banessa of Branston	B	Ch. Nice Fella of Wynsolot	Baffin of Branston	Mrs D. M. Dennis	Mrs D. M. Dennis	3-6-56
Bavena of Branston	B	Ch. Banker of Branston	Famecheck Teresa	Mrs D. M. Dennis	Mrs V. Hanks	28-5-58
Broomlaw Brandy	D	Eriegael Fabian O' Petriburg	Crystone Constance	Mrs M. B. Law	Mrs M. B. Law	21-1-57

Name	Sex	Sire	Dam	Owner	Breeder	Born
1959—contd. Citrus Warbler	D	Ch. Famecheck Jolly Warrior	Famecheck Cygnet	Mrs M. Lemon	Mrs M. Lemon	14-1-57
Cruben Happy	B	Calluna Big Wig	Cruben Elsa	Dr & Mrs A. Russell	Dr & Mrs A. Russell	11-5-57
Eriegael Mercedes	D	Ch. Kirnbrae Symmetra Sailaway	Eriegael	Miss J. Brown	Miss J. Brown	8-3-56
Famecheck Jolly Warrior	D	Ch. Famecheck Happy Knight	Int. Ch. Famecheck Lucky Charm	Miss F. M. C. Cook	Miss F. M. C. Cook	25-2-55
Furzefield Pickwick	D	Wolvey Postboy	Furzefield Picture	Mrs D. P. Allom	Mrs D. P. Allom	3-9-57
Phrana O' Petriburg	B	Calluna Big Wig	Phil O' Petriburg	Mrs A. Beels	Mrs A. Beels	23-6-58
Wolvey Palor	D	Ch. Wolvey Pirate	Wolvey Padella	Mrs C. Pacey	Mrs C. Pacey	23-5-57
Wolvey Pipers Tune	D	Ch. Wolvey Pied Piper	Ch. Wolvey Peach	Mrs C. Pacey	Mrs C. Pacey	23-6-57
Wolvey Postgirl	B	Ch. Wolvey Postmaster	Slitrig Spangle	Mrs C. Pacey	Mrs Kirby	30-9-57
1960 Bandsman of Branston	D	Ch. Banker of Branston	Ch. Banessa of Branston	Mrs D. M. Dennis	Mrs D. M. Dennis	27-9-58
Broomheather Freesia	B	Ch. Famecheck Jolly Roger	Ch. Broomheather Fianna	Mrs E. Hay	Mrs E. Hay	15-11-57
Eriegael Storm Child	B	Ch. Kirnbrae Symmetra Sailaway	Eriegael Martinette	Miss J. Brown	Miss J. Brown	11-1-59
Famecheck Gay Buccaneer	D	Ch. Famecheck Gay Crusader	Ch. Famecheck Lucky Mascot	Miss F. M. C. Cook	Miss F. M. C. Cook	12-4-59
Famecheck Joy	B	Ch. Famecheck Lucky Choice	Ch. Famecheck	Miss F. M. C. Cook	Miss F. M. C. Cook	9-1-55

130

Name	Sex	Sire	Dam	Breeder	Owner	Date
Famecheck Musketeer	D	Ch. Famecheck Gay Crusader	Ch. Famecheck Lucky Mascot	Miss F. M. C. Cook	Miss F. M. C. Cook	20-7-56
Glengyle Tapestry	B	Ch. Famecheck Gay Crusader	Ch. Freshney Fray	Mrs P. Welch	Mrs P. Welch	10-7-57
Stoneygap Flash	B	Ch. Furzefield Provost	Sheila Delight	Mrs G. M. Barr	Mr Hewett	12-7-59
Symmetra Skirmish	D	Tulyers Boy	Famecheck Lucky Star	Miss J. Brown	Mr & Mrs H. Mitchell	24-4-56
Wolvey Pavlova	B	Ch. Wolvey Palor	Wolvey Peewit	Mrs C. Pacey	Mrs C. Pacey	20-1-57
Wolvey Playgirl	B	Ch. Wolvey Pirate	Wolvey Padella	Mrs C. Pacey	Mrs C. Pacey	23-5-57
Workman of Wynsolot	D	Ch. Nice Fella of Wynsolot	Sally Ann of Wynsolot	Mrs E. A. Green	Mrs E. A. Green	17-10-58
1961 Brenda of Branston	B	Ch. Sollershott Sun-up	Ch. Brindie of Branston	Mrs D. M. Dennis	Mrs D. M. Dennis	1-2-60
Broomheather Fleur de Lis	B	Ch.Kirnbrae Symmetra Sailaway	Ch. Broomheather Fianna	Mrs E. Hay	Mrs E. Hay	20-6-58
Buttons of Helmsleigh	B	Ch. Furzefield Pickwick	Snowey Fee	Mrs G. M. Barr	Mr Rowland	4-3-59
Glengyle Thistle	B	Ch. Eriegal Mercedes	Ch. Glengyle Tapestry	Mrs P. M. Welch	Mrs P. M. Welch	23-5-58
Phancy O' Petriburg	B	Phryne O' Petriburg	Junyer Julie	Mrs A. Beels	Mr & Mrs L. A. Thomson	29-12-59
The Prior of Raventofts	D	Ch. Calluna the Laird	Pippa of Raventofts	Mrs N. Whitworth	Mrs N. Whitworth	7-3-60
Wolvey Permit	D	Ch. Wolvey Pipers Tune	Wolvey Pennywise	Mrs C. Pacey	Mrs C. Pacey	23-6-59
Wolvey Pickwick	D	Ch. Wolvey Pipers Tune	Wolvey Padella	Mrs C. Pacey	Mrs C. Pacey	13-2-59
1962 Alpin of Kendrum	D	Quakertown Quizzical	Pixie of Kendrum	Hon T. H. Rollo	Hon T. H. Rollo	13-4-61

Name	Sex	Sire	Dam	Owner	Breeder	Born
1962—contd. Banner of Branston	B	Ch. Banker of Branston	Bono of Branston	Mrs D. M. Dennis	Mrs D. M. Dennis	4-9-59
Banny of Branston	B	Ch. Banker of Branston	Bono of Branston	Mrs D. M. Dennis	Mrs D. M. Dennis	18-10-60
Birkfell Sea Shanty	B	Ch. Famecheck Jolly Roger	Birkfell Schottische	Miss S. Cleland	Miss S. Cleland	29-10-59
Birkfell Solitaire	B	Ch. Famecheck Jolly Roger	Birkfell Snowstorm	Miss S. Cleland	Miss S. Cleland	10-4-59
Famecheck Madcap	B	Ch. Famecheck Gay Crusader	Ch. Famecheck Lucky Mascot	Miss F. M. C. Cook	Miss F. M. C. Cook	20-10-59
Slitrig Sachet	B	Ch. Wolvey Postmaster	Slitrig Spangle	Mrs C. M. Kirby & Mr L. Pearson	Mrs C. M. Kirby	28-8-58
Sollershot Soloist	D	Ch. Bandsman of Branston	Citrus Silhouette	Mrs D. J. Kenney Taylor	Mrs D. J. Kenney Taylor	28-6-60
Stoneygap Bobbin of Gillobar	D	Bobbin of the Avenue	Stoneygap Rocky	Mr F. W. Fraser	Mrs G. M. Barr	10-8-60
Wolvey Punch	D	Ch. Wolvey Pipers Tune	Wolvey Peewit	Mrs C. Pacey	Mrs C. Pacey	15-6-60
1963 Billybong of Branston	D	Ch. Bandsman of Branston	June of Braddocks	Mrs D. M. Dennis	Mrs Pickess	11-2-61
Busybody of Branston	B	Ch. Sollershot Sun Up	Ch. Brindie of Branston	Mrs D. M. Dennis	Mrs D. M. Dennis	2-10-61
Lasara Lee	B	Lasara Laddie	Lasara Lassie	Mrs B. Graham & Mrs G. Hazell	Mrs B. Graham & Mrs G. Hazell	9-10-61
Petriburg Mark of Polteana	D	Ch. Calluna the Poacher	Whitebriar Jantie	Mrs A. Beels	Dr M. W. Beaver	22-9-60

Name	Sex	Sire	Dam	Breeder	Owner	Date
Slitrig Shiningstar of Lynwood	B	Ch. Famecheck Gay Buccaneer	Slitrig Sweet Suzette	Mr & Mrs G. Ellis	Mrs C. Kirby	16-12-61
Sollershot Symphony	B	Ch. Bandsman of Branston	Citrus Silhouette	Mrs J. Kenney-Taylor	Mrs J. Kenney-Taylor	28-6-60
Stoneygap Sugar Candy of Manraf	B	Ch. Workman of Wynsolot	Sugar Puff of Manraf	Mr F. W. Fraser	Mrs M. A. Farnham	26-4-62
Waideshouse Woodpecker	D	Waideshouse Wallaby	Waideshouse Wicked-ness	Mr & Mrs B. Thomson	Mr & Mrs B. Thomson	3-4-62
Whitebriar Jimolo	D	Ch. Famecheck Jolly Roger	Whitebriar Juna	Mrs J. E. Beer	Mrs J. E. Beer	22-1-60
Wolvey Paperman	D	Ch. Wolvey Pickwick	Wolvey Pipinella	Mrs C. Pacey	Mrs C. Pacey	14-11-61
1964 Baggage of Branston	B	Ch. Billybong of Branston	Becky of Branston	Mrs D. M. Dennis	Mrs D. M. Dennis	13-6-62
Citrus Lochinvar of Estcoss	D	Ch. Sollershot Sun-up	Famecheck Foxtrot	Mrs V. L. W. Estcourt	Mrs M. Lemon	5-9-59
Kandymint of Carryduff	B	Gillie of Carryduff	Sugarmint of Carry-duff	Mr J. C. Bell	Mr J. C. Bell	18-3-60
Mahgni Wooster	D	Ch. Calluna the Laird	Symmetra Symbol	Mr J. W. Stead	Mr A. Ingram	3-3-60
Rhianfa Rifleman	D	Rhianfa the Rock	Rhianfa Cheyenne Bodie	Mr F. N. Sills	Mrs A. Sagar	15-6-60
Rivelin Rhumba	B	Ch. Famecheck Gay Crusader	Rivelin Ragtime	Mr B. Osborne	Mrs M. Pearson	2-8-59
Snowcliff Spring Song	B	Ch. Calluna the Laird	Sweet Reality	Messrs Pearson & Berry	Mrs W. Pearson	14-3-61
Quakertown Quistador	D	Ch. Alpin of Kendrum	Quakertown Querida	Mrs K. Sansom	Mrs K. Sansom	26-12-63
Waideshouse Warrant	D	Ch. Petriburg Mark of Polteana	Waideshouse Wickedness	Mr & Mrs B. Thompson	Mr & Mrs B. Thompson	15-12-62

Name	Sex	Sire	Dam	Owner	Breeder	Born
1964—contd. Waideshouse Woodlark	B	Waideshouse Wallaby	Waideshouse Wickedness	Mr & Mrs B. Thomson	Mr & Mrs B. Thomson	3-4-62
1965 Bardel of Branston	D	Ch. Billybong of Branston	Ch. Banner of Branston	Mrs D. M. Dennis & Mrs R. K. Mellon	Mrs D. M. Dennis	16-6-63
Briarrose of Branston	B	Ch. Sollershot Sun Up	Ch. Brindie of Branston	Mrs D. M. Dennis & Mrs R. K. Mellon	Mrs D. M. Dennis	11-12-62
Glengyle Teasle	B	Ch. Sollershot Soloist	Ch. Glengyle Thistle	Mrs P. M. Welch	Mrs P. M. Welch	13-12-61
Phelo O' Petriburg	B	Ch. Petriburg Mark of Polteana	Phino O' Petriburg	Mrs E. A. Beels	Mrs E. A. Beels	2-2-63
Phluster O' Petriburg	B	Ch. Petriburg Mark of Polteana	Ch. Phancy O' Petriburg	Mrs E. A. Beels	Mrs E. A. Beels	22-9-62
Pillerton Pippa	B	Ch. Petriburg Mark of Polteana	Pillerton Pickle	Mrs S. J. Kearsey	Mrs S. J. Kearsey	15-5-63
Sollershot Freshney Foy	D	Ch. Sollershot Sun-up	Freshney Faggot	Mrs J. Kenney-Taylor	Mrs McKinney	26-8-63
Sollershot Sober	D	Ch. Sollershot Soloist	Sollershot Daybreak	Mrs J. Kenney-Taylor	Mrs J. Kenney-Taylor	14-9-63
1966 Alpinegay Impressario	D	Warberry Sattelite	Warberry Wideawake	Mrs B. Wheeler	Mrs B. Wheeler	20-1-65
Glengyle Blackpoint White Magic	B	Ch. Whitebriar Jimolo	Whitebriar Joris	Mrs P. Bird	Mrs P. M. Welch	11-3-62
Incheril Amarylis	B	Ch. Petriburg Mark of Polteana	Raasay Spry	Mr C. W. Berry	Mr C. W. Berry	27-9-62
Monsieur aus der	D	Int. Ch. Barnstormer of	Daggy Hallodri	Miss B. Zakschewski	Mr W. Flerlage	17-11-62

				Breeder	Owner	Date
1966—contd. Pillerton Peterman	D	Slitrig Simon of Lynwood	Pillerton Puckle	Mrs S. J. Kearsey	Mrs S. Kearsey	16-5-64
Pillerton Pippa	B	Ch. Petriburg Mark of Polteana	Pillerton Pickle	Mrs. S. J. Kearsey	Mrs S. Kearsey	15-5-63
1967 Birkfell Seafire	B	Ch. Kirnbrae Symmetra Sailaway	Ch. Birkfell Sea Shanty	Miss S. Cleland	Miss S. Cleland	4-10-62
Famecheck Hallmark	D	Famecheck Marksman	Famecheck Caprice	Miss F. M. C. Cook	Miss F. M. C. Cook	16-1-64
Famecheck Bernard	D	Famecheck Hallmark	Famecheck Banshee	Miss F. M. C. Cook and Dr Silfvast	Miss F. M. C. Cook	25-7-65
Famecheck Dainty Maid	B	Ch. Famecheck Hallmark	Famecheck Juliet	Miss F. M. C. Cook	Miss F. M. C. Cook	20-4-65
Glengyle Trader	D	Glengyle Tweed	Glengyle Tansy	Mrs P. M. Welch	Mrs P. M. Welch	3-8-61
Highstile Prank	D	Ch. Sollershot Soloist	Wolvey Puffin	Mrs M. Bertram	Mrs M. Bertram	6-5-64
Highstile Poppet	B	Ch. Quakertown Quistador	Wolvey Puppin	Mrs M. Bertram	Mrs M. Bertram	10-2-66
Lasara Louise	B	Ch. Lasara Liegeman	Lasara Lydia	Mrs B. Graham and Mrs G. Hazell	Mrs B. Graham and Mrs G. Hazell	29-7-64
Masquerade of Bamburgh	B	Warberry Satellite	My Lady of Bamburgh	Mrs M. A. Beesley	Mrs M. A. Beesley	8-9-65
Morenish Geordie	D	Ch. Sollershot Freshney Froy	Morenish Jane	Mrs G. Wallace	Miss E. C. Grieve	21-1-66
Pinkholme Paramount	D	Ch. Citrus Lochinvar of Estcoss	Pinkholme Promise	Mrs I. Dickinson	Mrs I. Dickinson	2-2-63
Slitrig Goshell of Branston	D	Ch. Billybong of Branston	Slitrig Sweet Suzette	Mrs D. M. Dennis	Mrs C. Kirby	15-4-65

Name	Sex	Sire	Dam	Owner	Breeder	Born
1967—contd. Snow Goblin	D	Rivelin Rector	Rayon Mill Penny	Mrs M. Hampson	Mr S. Allen	6-11-61
Strathairlie Swiss Miss	B	Ch. Bandsman of Branston	Strathairlie Starmist	Mrs M. Black	Mrs M. Black	24-9-62
Woodpuddle Bumble	B	Glengyle Tweed	Woodpuddle Wizz	Mrs C. Ingram	Mrs C. Ingram	8-8-60
1968 Alpinegay Sonata	D	Warberry Satellite	Warberry Wideawake	Miss C. Owen	Mrs. B. Wheeler	11-8-66
Famecheck Trojan	D	Ch. Famecheck Hallmark	Ch. Famecheck Verona	Miss F. M. C. Cook	Miss F. M. C. Cook	3-3-65
Famecheck Maid to Order	B	Ch. Famecheck Hallmark	Famecheck Helen	Miss F. M. C. Cook	Miss F. M. C. Cook	22-7-66
Lindenhall Discord	D	Ch. Citrus Warbler	Rainsborowe Bridie	Miss R. J. Fisher	Miss R. J. Fisher	4-3-66
Renlim Rachael	B	Ch. Sollershot Soloist	Wolvey Pardon Me	Mr and Mrs W. H. Milner	Miss R. J. Fisher	23-1-66
Rhianfa Up and Coming of Estcoss	B	Ch. Citrus Lochinvar of Estcoss	Rhianfa Rainsborowe Poppea	Mrs V. L. W. Estcourt	Mrs A. M. Sagar	27-7-64
Waideshouse Waterboy	D	Ch. Waideshouse Wiloughby	Ch. Waideshouse Woodlark	Mr and Mrs B. Thompson	Mr and Mrs B. Thompson	23-8-64
Whitebriar Jillan	B	Can. Ch. Whitebriar Jamie	Whitebriar Jatoma	Mrs M. Coy	Mrs J. E. Beer	12-5-63
1968 Glengyle Tuggles	B	Ch. Billybong of Branston	Ch. Glengyle Tapestry	Mrs P. Welch	Mrs P. Welch	23-7-63
Quakertown Querida	B	Quakertown Quarrelsome	Cara of Kendrum	Mrs K. Sansom	Mrs K. Sansom	9-10-60

1969						
Birkfell Solace	B	Ch. Pillerton Peterman	Ch. Birkfell Solitaire	Miss S. Cleland	Miss S. Cleland	16-5-66
Birkfell Solitude	B	Ch. Pillerton Peterman	Ch. Birkfell Solitaire	Miss S. Cleland	Miss S. Cleland	10-9-67
Checkbar Remony Rye	B	Broomheather	Brox Sundae	Mrs J. Taylor	Mrs E. Currie	3-9-65
Checkbar Donsie Kythe	D	Parkendcot Bobby Dazzler	Ch. Checkbar Remony Rye	Mrs J. Taylor	Mrs J. Taylor	23-11-67
Famecheck Sterling	B	Ch. Famecheck Hallmark	Famecheck Banshee	Miss F. Cook	Miss F. Cook	28-6-67
Famecheck Fashion Plate	B	Famecheck Man o' Mark	Famecheck Filibuster	Miss F. Cook and Mr P. Newman	Miss F. Cook	1-6-68
Glengyle Taiho	B	Ch. Bandsman of Branston	Ch. Glengyle Tapestry	Mrs P. Welch	Mrs P. Welch	22-9-62
Highstile Priceless	B	Ch. Alpin of Kendrum	Highstyle Pernickety	Mrs M. Bertram	Mrs M. Bertram	13-4-67
Lorrell's Last Legacy	D	The Squire of Cardona	Lorrell Treasure	Mrs M. Duell	Mrs M. Duell	25-12-67
Lindenhall Drambuie	D	Ch. Sollershott Soloist	Rainborowe Bridie	Mrs Millen	Mrs R. Beaver	15-1-65
Lindenhall Donna	B	Ch. Citrus Warbler	Rainsborowe Bridie	Miss R. Fisher & Mr J. Wilson	Miss R. Fisher	4-3-66
Quakertown Quandry	D	Ch. Quakertown Quistator	Quakertown Queen	Mrs K. Sansom	Mrs K. Sansom	9-5-67
1970						
Ceadarfell Messenger Dove	B	Whitebriar Jackson	Ch. Whitebriar Jillan	Mrs H. Painting	Mrs M. Coy	7-8-67
Famecheck Air Hostess	B	Ch. Famecheck Trojan	Famecheck Rowena	Miss F. Cook	Miss F. Cook	11-7-67

Name	Sex	Sire	Dam	Owner	Breeder	Born
1970—contd. Heath of Backmuir	D	Ch. Sollershott Freshney	Highstile Pick Up	Mr & Mrs Gellan	Mr & Mrs Gellan	21-6-67
Rosyles Promise	D	Ch. Quakertown Quandry	Highstile Prim	Mrs S. Wood	Mrs S. Wood	5-10-68
Sumar Glengyle Tucket	B	Ch. Glengyle Trader	Ch. Glengyle Tuggles	Miss S. Jackson	Mrs P. Welch	25-10-67
Thornesian Marquis	D	Rocket Ranrou	Thornesian Cologyne	Mr & Mrs L. Haynes	Mr & Mrs L. Haynes	12-7-68
1971 Bradbury of Branston	D	Bartel of Branston	Blue Velvet of Branston	Mrs D. M. Dennis	Mrs D. M. Dennis	27-8-66
Ballacoar Musetta of Cedarfell	B	Whitebriar Jackson	Ch. Whitebriar Jillan	Mrs S. Morgan	Mrs M. Coy	28-4-69
Birkfell Something Stupid	B	Ch. Macnab of Balmaha	Ch. Birkfell Solace	Miss S. Cleland	Miss S. Cleland	7-1-68
Cedarfell Merry 'n Bright	D	Cedarfell Man o' Minx	Cedarfell Minuet	Mrs M. Coy	Mrs M. Coy	14-2-70
Famecheck Glamis	B	Ch. Famecheck Hallmark	Shadwin Shanto Bella	Miss F. Cook	Miss F. Cook	8-5-69
Incheril Inge	B	Halfmerke Monarch	Incheril Ilex	Mrs C. Berry	Mrs C. Berry	25-1-69
Pillerton Peterkin	D	Ch. Pillerton Peterman	Pillerton Polka	Mrs S. Kearsey	Mrs S. Kearsey	29-1-68
Seelaw Selena	B	Ch. Macnab of Balmaha	Betsy May of Balmaha	Mrs G. Corish	Mrs G. Corish	16-12-67
Checkbar Tommy Quite Right	D	Ch. Alpin of Kendrum	Ch. Checkbar Remoney Rye	Mrs J. Taylor	Mrs J. Taylor	20-4-69
Whitebriar Jonfair	D	Whitebriar Jannock	Whitebriar Jeeny	Mr J. Hodsall	Mrs J. Beer	1-6-70
1972 Birkfell Sea Squall	D	Ch. Quakertown Quandry	Birkfell Sea Fury	Miss S. Cleland	Miss S. Cleland	20-11-70

138

1972—contd.						
Birkfell Solicitude	B	Ch. Famecheck Hallmark	Ch. Birkfell Solicitude	Miss S. Cleland	Miss S. Cleland	18-12-68
Famecheck Busybody	B	Ch. Famecheck Hallmark	Famecheck Wellmaid	Miss F. Cook	Miss F. Cook	7-11-70
Lasara Limpet	B	Ch. Pillerton Peterman	Lasara Limit	Mrs B. Graham & Hazell	Mrs B. Graham & Hazell	27-1-67
Melwyn Pillerton Picture	B	Eriegael Storm Warning	Ch. Pillerton Pippa	Mrs R. Pritchard	Mrs S. Kearsey	30-8-68
Medalist of Cedarfell	D	Provost o' Petriburg	Ch. Whitebriar Jillan	Mrs B. Armstrong	Mrs M. Coy	14-10-68
Rhianfa Take Notice	D	Lymehills Birkfell South Pacific	Rhianfa Lady Constance of Estcoss	Miss C. Owen	Mrs A. Sagar	24-2-69
Sarmac Heathstream Drummer Boy	D	Ch. Lindenhall Drambuie	Heathstream Cedarfell Misty Dell	Mrs A. Millen	Mrs Farnes	11-5-69
Tasman March of Time	D	Ch. Highstile Prank	Pillerton Pollyann	Mrs C. Bonas	Mrs C. Bonas	21-9-68
Tasman Adoration	B	Tasman Temptation	Tasman Beau	Mrs C. Bonas	Mrs C. Bonas	8-8-70
White Rose of Ide	B	Ch. Heath of Backmuir	Gala of Backmuir	Mr P. Newman	Mr & Mrs Gellan	26-7-70
1973						
Gaywyn Gypsy	B	Ch. Apinegay Sonata	Ch. Phelo O' Petriburg	Miss C. Owen	Mrs E. A. Beels	24-6-69
Clantarton Chrysanthemum	B	Clantarton Carnog Crest	Clantarton Calla Pippa	Mrs J. Blakey	Mrs J. Blakey	19-6-69
Lasara Linda Belle	B	Ch. Pillerton Peterman	Lasara Lydia	Mrs B. Graham & Mrs G. Hazell	Mrs B. Graham & Mrs G. Hazell	26-10-65
Pillerton Prejudice	B	Ch. Pillerton Peterman	Birkfell Screech Owl	Mrs S. Kearsey	Mr M. Collings	21-4-71
Halfmarke Marina	B	Toibeech White Cockade	Halfmerke Moonbeam	Mr G. D. Green	Mr G. D. Green	9-11-70

Name	Sex	Sire	Dam	Owner	Breeder	Born
1973—contd. Drumcope Dewdrop	B	Ch. Checkbar Donsie Kythe	Drumcope Bonnie	Mrs N. Copeland	Mrs N. Copeland	23-8-70
Nailbourne Nutcracker	B	Ch. Lindenhall Discord	Quakertown Quincella	Mrs H. Davies	Mrs L. B. Bell	6-7-69
Easter Bonnetina	B	Rivelin Jock	Samantha of the Highlands	Mrs B. Pogson	Mr G. Lancaster	2-4-69
Commander of Tintibar	D	Ch. Checkbar Donsie Kythe	Sally of Clyndarose	Mr & Mrs H. S. Brittain	Mrs. E. Brittain	30-4-69
Gaywyn Bradey of Branston	D	Ch. Alpinegay Sonata	Beautiful Biddy of Branston	Miss C. Owen	Mrs D. M. Dennis	27-6-69
Ardenrun Andsome of Purston	D	Ch. Whitebriar Jonfair	Ardenrun Agitator	Mr M. Collings	Mr C. Oakley	18-6-72
Purston Petite	B	Ch. Pillerton Peterman	Birkfell Screech Owl	Mr A. Parr	Mr M. Collings	21-4-71
Glengordon Finearte Prince of Peace	D	Ch. Sarmac Heathstream Drummer Boy	Ch. Cedarfell Messenger Dove	Mrs K. Budden	Mrs H. Painting	14-11-70
Cedarfell Moon Melody	B	Ch. Lindenhall Drambuie	Cedarfell Minuet	Mr R. Armstrong	Mrs M. Coy	3-7-69
1974 Birkfell Soliloquy	B	Ch. Famecheck Hallmark	Ch. Birkfell Solitude	Miss S. Cleland	Miss S. Cleland	16-12-68
Checkbar Findley McDougal	D	Ch. Checkbar Donsie Kythe	Happy Sheila Bella	Mrs J. Taylor	Mrs J. Taylor	30-8-71
Milburn Mandy	B	Ch. Quakertown Quandary	Milburn Melody	Mr N. Herbison	Mr N. Herbison	29-10-71
Dianthus Buttons	D	Ch. Alpin of Kendrum	Starcyl Sioux	Mrs Newstead	Mrs Newstead	1-1-72

1974—*contd.*						
Furzeleigh Last Edition	B	Ch. Rhianfa's Take Notice	Whitebriar Jeenay	Mr J. Hodsoll	Mr J. Hodsoll	17-11-72
Olac Moonraker	D	Pillerton Perry	Miranda of Olac	Mr D. Tattersall	Mr D. Tattersall	3-4-73
Famecheck Silver Charm	B	Ch. Famecheck Hallmark	Ch. Famecheck Air Hostess	Miss F. Cook	Miss F. Cook	16-4-73
Birkfell Silver Thistle of Clanestar	B	Ch. Birkfell Sea Squall	Ch. Birkfell Solitude	Mrs D. K. Lancaster	Miss S. Cleland	15-1-72
Purston Peter Pan	D	Ch. Pillerton Peterman	Birkfell Screech Owl	Mr. M. Collings	Mr. M. Collings	24-11-72
Eriscort Special Request	D	Ch. Quakertown Quandry	Eriscort Domaroy Debutante	Mr R. Hodgkinson	Mr R. Hodgkinson	2-7-72
Drumcope Teddy Tar	D	Ch. Checkbar Donsie Kythe	Drumcope Bonnie	Mrs N. Copeland	Mrs N. Copeland	23-8-70
Lucky of Loughore	D	Glentromie Peter	Lupin of Loughore	Mr J. S. Madill	Mr J. S. Madill	23-5-70
1975						
Candida of Crinan	B	Selig Rustin of Crinan	Highstile Pixie	Mrs B. Hands	Mr Clay	4-9-72
Melwyn Milly Molly Mandy	B	Cedarfell Man O' Minx	Ch. Melwyn Pillerton Picture	Mrs. R. Pritchard	Mrs R. Pritchard	30-12-71
Binate Inveraray	D	Braidholme White Tornado of Binate	Drumcope Starry Mist	Mr & Mrs Haverhand	Mrs Copeland	26-10-71
Robbie McGregor of Wyther Park	D	Nolstar Snowstorm	Nolstar Patine	Miss A. Garnett	Mr Schmidt	9-8-71
Carillyon Cadence	B	Ch. Cedarfell Merry-N-Bright	Whitebriar Jamanda	Mrs. T. M. Lees	Mrs T. M. Lees	24-2-72
Justrite Jacinda	B	Ch. Medallist of Cedarfell	Ch. Cedarfell Moon Melody	Mr & Mrs R. Armstrong	Mr & Mrs R. Armstrong	7-5-73

Name	Sex	Sire	Dam	Owner	Breeder	Born
1975—contd.						
Ballacoar Samantha	B	Cedarfell Man-O-Minx	Blackpoynt Blythe Spirit	Mrs P. Graham	Mrs S. Morgan	29–9–72
Glenalwyne Sonny Boy	D	Ch. Cedarfell Merry-N-Bright	Clynebury Silver Kilt	Miss J. Herbert	Miss J. Herbert	20–3–73
Glengordon Hannah	B	Ch. Glengordon Fine-arte Prince of Peace	Glengordon Suzette	Mrs M. Torbet	Mrs H. Budden	8–12–71
Yelrav Spangle	B	Yelrav Gay Marquis	Yelrav Scorcha	Mr & Mrs Brownhill	Mr & Mrs E. Varley	5–10–72
Incheril at Large	D	Ch. Checkbar Donsie Kythe	Incheril Ispedixit	Mr C. Berry	Mr C. Berry	8–1–74

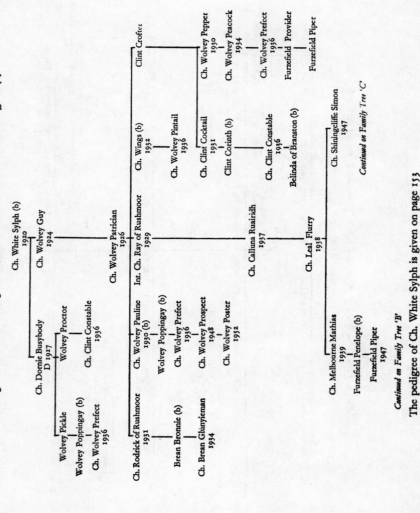

Family Tree 'A'. Mainly male, all bitches included have the suffix (b)

Ch. White Sylph (b)
1920

Ch. Wolvey Guy
1924

Ch. Dornie Busybody
D 1927

Wolvey Pickle

Wolvey Poppingay (b)

Ch. Wolvey Prefect
1936

Wolvey Proctor

Ch. Clint Constable
1936

Ch. Wolvey Patrician
1926

Ch. Wolvey Pauline
1930 (b)

Wolvey Poppingay (b)

Ch. Wolvey Prefect
1936

Ch. Wolvey Prospect
1948

Ch. Wolvey Poster
1932

Ch. Rodrick of Rushmoor
1931

Brean Bronnie (b)

Ch. Brean Glunyieman
1934

Int. Ch. Ray of Rushmoor
1929

Ch. Wings (b)
1932

Ch. Wolvey Pintail
1936

Ch. Clint Cocktail
1931

Clint Corinth (b)

Ch. Clint Constable
1936

Belinda of Branston (b)

Clint Crofter

Ch. Wolvey Peppet
1930

Ch. Wolvey Peacock
1934

Ch. Wolvey Prefect
1936

Furzefield Provider

Furzefield Piper

Ch. Calluna Ruairidh
1937

Ch. Leal Flurry
1938

Ch. Melbourne Mathias
1939

Furzefield Penelope (b)

Furzefield Piper
1947

Ch. Shiningcliffe Simon
1947

Continued on Family Tree 'C'

Continued on Family Tree 'B'

The pedigree of Ch. White Sylph is given on page 153

Family Tree 'B'. Mainly male, all bitches included have the suffix (b)

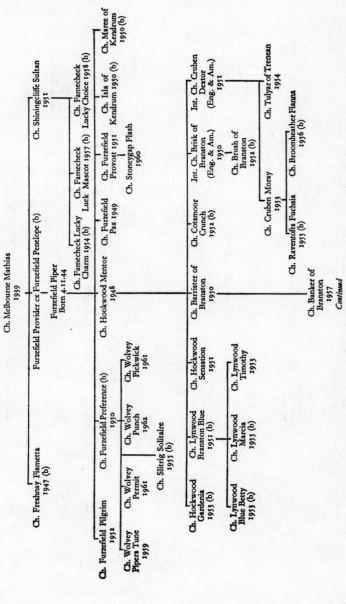

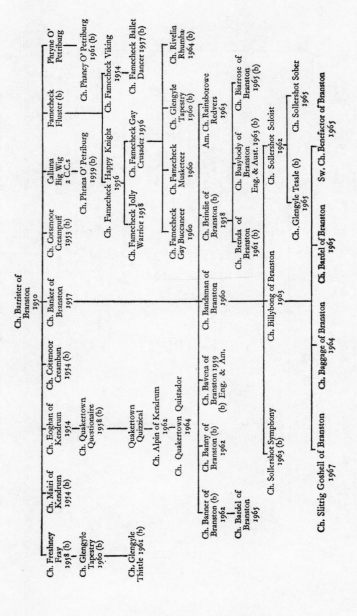

Family Tree 'C'. Mainly male, all bitches included have the suffix (b)

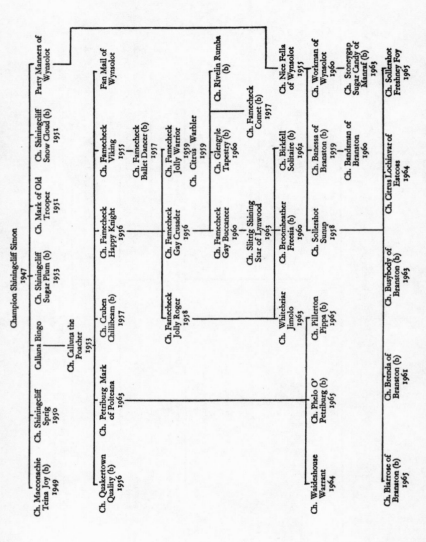

Champion Shiningcliff Simon
1947

Parry Manners of Wynsolot

Ch. Macconachie Teina Joy (b) 1949 — Ch. Shiningcliff Sprig 1950 — Calluna Bingo — Ch. Shiningcliff Sugar Plum (b) 1953 — Ch. Mark of Old Trooper 1951 — Ch. Shiningcliff Snow Cloud (b) 1951

Ch. Calluna the Poacher 1953

Fan Mail of Wynsolot

Ch. Quakertown Quality (b) 1956 — Ch. Cruben Chillibeam (b) 1957 — Ch. Famecheck Happy Knight 1956 — Ch. Famecheck Viking 1955

Ch. Famecheck Ballet Dancer (b) 1957

Ch. Famecheck Jolly Warrior 1959

Ch. Citrus Warbler 1959

Ch. Petriburg Mark of Polteana 1963 — Ch. Famecheck Jolly Roger 1958 — Ch. Famecheck Gay Crusader 1956 — Ch. Glengyle Tapestry (b) 1960

Ch. Rivelin Rumba (b)

Ch. Famecheck Comet (b) 1957

Ch. Famecheck Gay Buccaneer 1960

Ch. Slitrig Shining Star of Lynwood 1963

Ch. Nice Fella of Wynsolot

Ch. Workman of Wynsolot 1960

Ch. Stoneygap Sugar Candy of Manraf (b) 1963

Whitebriar Jimolo — Ch. Broomheather Freesia (b) 1960 — Ch. Birkfell Solitaire (b) 1962 — Ch. Banessa of Branston (b) 1959

Ch. Bandsman of Branston 1960

Waidshouse Warrant 1964 — Ch. Phelo O' Petriburg (b) 1965 — Ch. Pillerton Pippa (b) 1965 — Ch. Sollershot Sunup 1958 — Ch. Citrus Lochinvar of Eatcote 1964 — Ch. Sollershot Freshney Foy 1965

Ch. Biarrose of Branston (b) 1965 — Ch. Brenda of Branston (b) 1961 — Ch. Busybody of Branston (b) 1963

146

Copy of the breed classes at the Kennel Club Show held October 1913. *Judge:* Mr John Lee.

Puppy Class 476—Dogs
First Prize £3   Second Prize £2   Third Prize £1

1286   Mrs Cecil Clare. WALPOLE WISEACRE. Born Dec. 25th 1912. Breeder exhibitor. By Ch. Morven—Walpole Witch.

1287   Miss Ruth Boyd. LAIRD O'BRITTONIA. Born May 16th 1913. Breeder Mr Holland Buckley. By Ch. Scotia Chief—Katty. Not for sale.

1288   Miss E. Tanner. ADAM. Born Feb. 18th 1913. By Ch. Morova—Lillah. Breeder exhibitor.

1289   Mr W. H. Baker. THANET BARLOW. Born March 8th 1913. Breeder exhibitor. By Ch. Morova—Thaner Creolag. Price £20

1290   Mr A. Baird. BIRCHFIELD LEADER. Age unknown. Breeder Mr J. Campbell. By Ornsay Slogan—Ornsay Nanny.

1291   Miss W. Buckley. SCOTIA FOREVER. Born Jan. 29th 1913. Breeder exhibitor. By Ch. Cairn Ransa—Scotia Spearwort. Price £150.

1292   Mr J. Firth. MEANWOOD ADMIRAL. Born Jan. 28th 1913. By Kingsborough—Star of the North. Breeder exhibitor. Price £50.

1293   Mr W. Glaisby. ORNSAY DEFENDER. Born Feb. 27th 1913. Breeder exhibitor. Ornsay Slogan—Ornsay Tinny. Price £200.

1294   Mrs E. Bullen-Smith. WESTWARD BILLY. Born Jan. 31st 1913. Breeder exhibitor. By Lothian Pride—Snow Fairey. Price £78.

1295   The Hon. Mrs Gerald Lascelles. LYNDHURST BADGER. Born March 7th 1913. Breeder exhibitor. By Moresco—Lyndhurst Polly.

Maiden Class 477—Dogs

1296 Mr E. G. Trump. ACE OF SPADES. Born Oct. 2nd 1912.
Breeder exhibitor. By Chief of Childwick—Deuce of
Diamonds. Price £42 10s.

1297 Mr W. E. Gray. ROWLAND. Born Sept. 8th 1912. Breeder
Mr A. Furness. By Strathmore—Lassie.

1298 Mr R. Cooke. GUYON. Born March 10th 1913. Breeder Miss
McQueen. By Ensay—Callac.

(1286) Mrs Cecil Clare. WALPOLE WISEACRE.

(1287) Miss Ruth Boyd. LAIRD O'BRITTONIA.

(1290) Mr A. Baird. BIRCHFIELD LEADER.

(1291) Miss W. Buckley. SCOTIA FOREVER.

(1292) Mr J. Firth. MEANWOOD ADMIRAL.

(1293) Mr W. Glaisby. ORNSAY DEFENDER.

(1295) The Hon. Mrs Gerald Lascelles. LYNDHURST BADGER.

Graduate Class No. 479—Dogs

First Prize £3   Second Prize £2   Third Prize £1

1299 Mr O. Every. MORIS. Born Dec. 16th 1911. Breeder Mrs
Hunter. By Ch. Morova—Mingle.

1300 Mr A. Graham. DUNVEGAN RASCAL. Born May 10th 1911.
Breeder Mr S. McLeod. By Dunvegan Hero—Lassie.

1301 Mrs A. Hume Binney. SPARK OF THE GREENWAY. Born April
18th 1912. Breeder exhibitor. By Mallaig—Thistledown.

1302 Mr G. Renwick, Jnr. REPTON RECRUIT. Born Aug. 15th 1912.
Breeder Mr B. Cowell. By Sparkling King—Yum. Price
£75.

(1288) Mrs E. Tanner. ADAM.

(1290) Mr A. Baird. BIRCHFIELD LEADER.

(1291) Miss W. Barber. SCOTIA FOREVER.

(1293) Mr W. Glaisby. ORNSAY DEFENDER.

(1295) The Hon. Mrs Gerald Lascelles. LYNDHURST DEFENDER.

Limit Class No. 480—Dogs

First Prize £3   Second Prize £2   Third Prize £1

1303 Mr G. Renwick, Jnr. REPTON HARD NUT. Born May 27th
1912. Breeder Mr E. Mullard. By Ornsay Slogan—Cressage
Primrose. Price £75.

1305 Miss F. Mackenzie. LOTHIAN DEFENDER. Born Jan. 5th 1912.
Breeder Mr A. Hume. By Ch. Cairn Nevis—Lothian
Beauty.

1308 Mrs C. Pacey. WOLVEY MACNAB. Born June 28th 1911.
Breeder Mrs H. Shawe. By Atholl—Weddington Sanna.

1309 Mrs E. Tanner. TINYMAN. Born June 28th 1912. Breeder
exhibitor. By Ch. Morova—Lillah.

1310 Mr H. Barrett. TERRABYRUCH. Born Nov. 12th 1910.
Breeder exhibitor. By Trenmore—Melford Judith.

1312 Mrs M. A. Logan. JUPITER SANDS. Born July 1911. Breeder
Mr G. Collin. By Hillsman Sands—Kitty Sands.

1313 Mr E. Mullard. CRAFTSMAN. Born March 5th 1912. Breeder
exhibitor. By Ornsay Thistle—Cressage Countess.

1314 Captain L. R. Peel. HOLMFIELD HERIOT. Born Nov. 11th
1910. Breeder Mr H. Barrett. By Trenmore—Melford
Judith.

1315 Mr Errington Ross. GLENHMOR PRIDE. Born Dec. 27th 1911.
Breeder Mrs Macdonald. By Dunvegan Heath—White
Witch. Price £250.

(1290) Mr A. Baird. BIRCHFIELD LEADER.

(1291) Miss W. Buckley. SCOTIA FOREVER.

(1299) Mr O. Every. MORIS.

(1300) Mr A. Graham. DUNVEGAN RASCAL.

(1301) Mrs A. Binney. SPARK OF THE GREENWAY.

Open Class No. 481—Dogs
First Prize £3   Second Prize £2   Third Prize £1

1304 Mr G. Renwick, Jnr. REPTON RECTOR. Born April 23rd 1911.
Breeder Mr C. Trevena. By Firth Grange Max—Firth
Grange Cracker. Price £105.

1316 Mrs Cecil Clare. Ch. CAIRN RANSA. Born May 8th 1911.
Breeder Mr C. Young. By Cairn Roe—Corry Lochan.

1317 Mrs L. A. Nicholson. HIGHLAND LEADER. Born May 3rd
1908. Breeder Mr Colin Young. By Rambler—Morag.

1318 Miss H. W. Roger. MAULDEN TOSKER. Born August 20th
1911. Breeder Commander Black. By Maulden Crofter—
Peggy.

(1290) Mr A. Baird. BIRCHFIELD LEADER.

(1291) Miss W. Buckley. SCOTIA FOREVER.

(1299) Mr O. Every. MORIS.

(1305) Miss F. Mackenzie. LOTHIAN DEFENDER.
(1308) Mrs C. Pacey. WOLVEY MACNAB.
(1309) Mr E. Tanner. TINYMAN.
(1310) Mr H. Barrett. TERRABYRUCH.
(1312) Mrs M. A. Logan. JUPITER SANDS.
(1313) Mr E. Mullard. CRAFTSMAN.
(1314) Captain L. R. Peel. HOLMFIELD HERIOT.
(1315) Mr Errington Ross. GLENHMOR PRIDE.

Puppy Class No. 482—Bitches
First Prize £3   Second Prize £2   Third Prize £1

1311 Mr H. Barrett. EIDERINE. Born Jan. 7th 1913. Breeder Mr J. McCullum. By Terrabyruch—Doran.

1319 Mrs Cecil Clare. WALPOLE WORRY. Born Nov. 2nd 1912. Breeder exhibitor. By Ch. Cairn Ransa.—Walpole Worry.

1320 Mr W. Glaisby. ORNSAY FROLIC. Born Nov. 23rd 1912. Breeder exhibitor. By Ch. Cairn Nansa—Ornsay Perfection. Price £100

1321 Mrs M. A. Logan. LANGTON MISTY. Born Dec. 6th 1912. Breeder Mr Fogg. By Cannoch—Love a Lassie.

1322 Captain L. R. Peel. HOLMFIELD HOPEFUL. Born Jan. 21st 1913. Breeder exhibitor. By Ch. Cairn Ransa—Corrylees.

1323 Captain L. R. Peel. HOLMFIELD HUSSY. Born Jan. 21st 1913. Breeder exhibitor. By Ch. Cairn Ransa—Corrylees.

1324 Mr G. Collin. BETTY SANDS. Born Jan. 28th 1913. Breeder exhibitor. By Hillsman Sands—Kitty Sands. Price £55.

1325 Mrs F. Hasslacher. CLEAVE MAVIS. Born Jan. 25th 1913. Breeder exhibitor. By Ch. Cairn Ransa—Dochfour Hectorina.

1326 Mrs P. Birkin. BLANTYRE MARTHA. Born Dec. 21st 1912. Breeder exhibitor. By Ch. Morova—Ch. Blantyre Minnie.

1327 Miss M. McBain. WYFOLD QUEEN. Born Nov. 25th 1912. Breeder exhibitor. By Adamant—Heilan Craigie. Price £100.

1328 Captain W. King Pierce. GENTLE JILL. Born March 6th 1913. Breeder Miss B. A. Melsome. By The White Chief—Jean.

1329 Mrs B. Lucas. KEPSTORN LARK. Born Nov. 4th 1912. Breeder Mr J. B. Hamilton. By Ch. Cairn Nevis—Skylark.

1330 Mrs M. S. Hunter. MORDKIN. Born April 5th 1913. Breeder Mr A. Galloway. By Monso—Myra.

1331 The Baroness Burton. DOCHFOUR MINA. Born Jan. 29th 1913.
Exhibitor. By Ch. Morova—Dochfour Spean.

1332 Mr L. Williams. LASSIE. Born March 28th 1913. Breeder Mr
C. Viccars. By Challenge of Childwick—Betty of Childwick.

Maiden Class No. 483—Bitches

First Prize £3   Second Prize £2   Third Prize £1

1333 Mr R. Cooke. GALATEA. Born March 10th 1913. Breeder
Miss McQueen. By Ensay—Callac.

1334 Mrs F. Hasslacher. CLEAVE METEOR. Born Jan. 25th 1913.
Breeder exhibitor. By Ch. Cairn Ransa—Dochfour Hectorina.

1335 Mr L. Williams. ROLLETTE OF CHILDWICK. Born June 7th
1911. Breeder Mr J. A. Cameron. By Chief of Childwick—
Queen.

(1320) Mr W. Glaisby. ORNSAY FROLIC.
(1321) Mrs M. A. Logan. LANGTON MISTY.
(1325) Mrs F. Hasslacher. CLEAVE MAVIS.
(1326) Mrs P. Birkin. BLANTYRE MARTHA.
(1330) Mrs M. S. Hunter. MORDKIN.

Novice Class No. 484—Bitches

First Prize £3   Second Prize £2   Third Prize £1

1306 Miss F. Mackenzie. ARDOCH PERFECTION. Born June 19th
1911. Breeder Mr J. Cairns. By Dunollie Chief—Mona.

1336 Mrs C. Pacey. WOLVET MIST. Born August 24th 1912.
Breeder exhibitor. By Ch. Scotia Chiel—Wolvey Thistle.
Price £25.

1337 Mrs C. Pacey. WOLVEY SPARK. Born August 28th 1912.
Breeder exhibitor. By Ch. Scotia Chiel—Wolvey Thistle.
Price £10.

1338 Mr E. G. Trump. TREY OF SPADES. Born Oct. 2nd 1912.
Breeder exhibitor. By Chief of Childwick—Deuce of
Diamonds. Price £42 10s.

1339 Miss H. W. Rogers. ROSEMARY OF GUNNERSBURY. Born
March 7th 1912. Breeder Mr E. G. Trump. By Alister Sands
—Deuce of Diamonds.

(1320) Mr W. Glaisby. ORNSAY FROLIC.
(1324) Mr G. Collin. BETTY SANDS.

(1325) Mrs F. Hasslacher. CLEAVE MAVIS.
(1329) Mrs B. Lucas. KEPSTORN LARK.

Graduate Class No. 485—Bitches
First Prize £3   Second Prize £2   Third Prize £1

1340 Mrs C. Pacey. WOLVEY BROOM. Born July 7th 1911. Breeder
      Mrs Turnbull. By Padraig—Carach of Childwick. Price £30.
(1306) Miss F. Mackenzie. ARDOCH PERFECTION.
(1324) Mr G. Collin. BETTY SANDS.
(1326) Mrs P. Birkin. BLANTYRE MARTHA.
(1327) Miss M. McBain. WYFOLD QUEEN.
(1338) Mr E. G. Trump. TREY OF SPADES.

Limit Class No. 486—Bitches
First Prize £3   Second Prize £2   Third Prize £1

1341 Mr A. Ellis. SAUCY O'SHANTER. Born Nov. 8th 1911. Breeder
      exhibitor. By Heilan Commander—Laughing Lassie.
1342 Mrs Cecil Clare. WALPOLE WAITRESS. Born Feb. 26th 1912.
      Breeder Mr D. Teage. By Alister Sands—Dudswell
      Mulaidh.
1343 Mr E. G. Trump. TREY OF CLUBS. Born March 7th 1912.
      Breeder exhibitor. By Alister Sands—Deuce of Diamonds.
      Price £55.
1344 Mr W. E. Gray. MAY BEAUTY. Born April 6th 1912. Breeder
      exhibitor. By Padraig—May Blossom.
1345 Mr C. Viccars. ROSALE OF CHILDWICK. Born Sept. 14th 1909.
      Breeder Mrs R. Martin. By Dunvegan Chief—Creuvack.
1346 Mrs Lionel Portman. SWAITES CULAIG. Born March 8th 1912.
      Breeder exhibitor. By Ch. Morova—Ch. Swaites Croachan.
(1306) Miss F. Mackenzie. ARDOCH PERFECTION.
(1327) Miss M. McBain. WYFOLD QUEEN.
(1340) Mrs C. Pacey. WOLVEY BROOM.

Open Class No. 487—Bitches
First Prize £3   Second Prize £2   Third Prize £1

1307 Miss F. Mackenzie. CROWN PRINCESS. Born Nov. 16th 1909.
      Breeder Mr M. McLellan. By Majestic—Suechda.

1347 Mrs Lionel Portman. Ch. SWAITES CRUACHAN. Born March 8th 1910. Breeder exhibitor. By Ch. Lagavulin—Swaites Clis.

(1306) Miss F. Mackenzie. ARDOCH PERFECTION.

(1327) Miss M. McBain. WYFOLD QUEEN.

(1341) Mr A. Ellis. SAUCY O'SHANTER.

(1342) Mrs Cecil Clare. WALPOLE WAITRESS.

(1344) Mr W. E. Gray. MAY BEAUTY.

(1345) Mr C. Viccars. ROSALIE OF CHILDWICK.

(1346) Mrs Lionel Portman. SWAITES CULAIG.

THE WEST HIGHLAND WHITE TERRIER CLUB OF ENGLAND

4th Produce—2nd Division

First Prize £8 15s.   Second Prize £2 10s.   Third Prize £1 5s.

(1327) Miss McBain. WYFOLD QUEEN.

(1336) Mrs C. Pacey. WOLVEY MIST.

(1337) Mrs C. Pacey. WOLVEY SPARK.

APPENDIX V

Eng. & Aust.: CHAMPION BUSYBODY OF BRANSTON and CHAMPION BRIARROSE OF BRANSTON

Sire
Ch. Sollershot Sun-up
- Ch. Nice Fella of Wynsolot
  - Fan Mail of Wynsolot
    - Party Manners of Wynsolot
    - Freedoms Fortune
  - Shiningcliff Starturn
    - Ch. Shiningcliff Sultan
    - Ch. Shiningcliff Dunthorne Damsel
- Cotsmoor Crack O' Dawn
  - Ch. Furzefield Pilgrim
    - Furzefield Piper
    - Furzefield Purpose
  - Cotsmoor Crusty
    - Ch. Wolvey Poster
    - Ch. Cotsmoor Crunch

Dam
Ch. Brindie of Branston
- Ch. Banker of Branston
  - Ch. Barrister of Branston
    - Ch. Hookwood Mentor
    - Bloom of Branston
  - Binty of Branston
    - Brigadier of Branston
    - Beau of Branston
- Bono of Branston
  - Ch. Barrister of Branston
    - Ch. Hookwood Mentor
    - Bloom of Branston
  - Cheeky Cherubim
    - Baron of Branston
    - Stort Bedelia

CHAMPION BARDEL OF BRANSTON

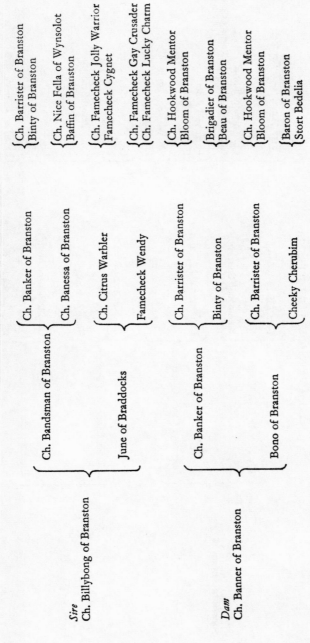

Sire
Ch. Billybong of Branston

Ch. Bandsman of Branston
{ Ch. Banker of Branston
  Ch. Banessa of Branston

June of Braddocks
{ Ch. Citrus Warbler
  Famecheck Wendy

Dam
Ch. Banner of Branston

Ch. Banker of Branston
{ Ch. Barrister of Branston
  Binty of Branston

Bono of Branston
{ Ch. Barrister of Branston
  Cheeky Cherubim

Ch. Banker of Branston
{ Ch. Barrister of Branston
  Binty of Branston

Ch. Banessa of Branston
{ Ch. Nice Fella of Wynsolot
  Baffin of Branston

Ch. Citrus Warbler
{ Ch. Famecheck Jolly Warrior
  Famecheck Cygnet

Famecheck Wendy
{ Ch. Famecheck Gay Crusader
  Ch. Famecheck Lucky Charm

Ch. Barrister of Branston
{ Ch. Hookwood Mentor
  Bloom of Branston

Binty of Branston
{ Brigadier of Branston
  Beau of Branston

Ch. Barrister of Branston
{ Ch. Hookwood Mentor
  Bloom of Branston

Cheeky Cherubim
{ Baron of Branston
  Stort Bedelia

CHAMPION SOLLERSHOT FRESHNEY FOY

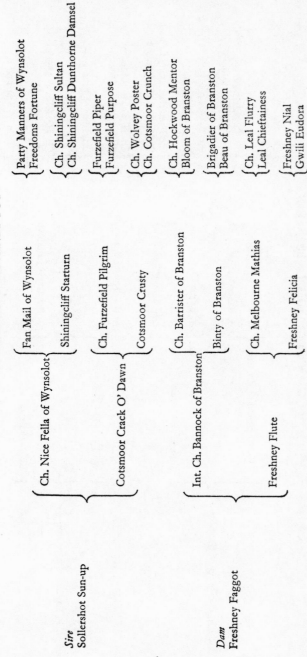

Sire
Sollershot Sun-up

Ch. Nice Fella of Wynsolot
{
  Fan Mail of Wynsolot
  {
    Party Manners of Wynsolot
    Freedoms Fortune
  }
  Shiningcliff Starturn
  {
    Ch. Shiningcliff Sultan
    Ch. Shiningcliff Dunthorne Damsel
  }
}

Cotsmoor Crack O' Dawn
{
  Ch. Furzefield Pilgrim
  {
    Furzefield Piper
    Furzefield Purpose
  }
  Cotsmoor Crusty
  {
    Ch. Wolvey Poster
    Ch. Cotsmoor Crunch
  }
}

Dam
Freshney Faggot

Int. Ch. Bannock of Branston
{
  Ch. Barrister of Branston
  {
    Ch. Hockwood Mentor
    Bloom of Branston
  }
  Binty of Branston
  {
    Brigadier of Branston
    Beau of Branston
  }
}

Freshney Flute
{
  Ch. Melbourne Mathias
  {
    Ch. Leal Flurry
    Leal Chieftainess
  }
  Freshney Felicia
  {
    Freshney Nial
    Gwili Eudora
  }
}

CHAMPION FAMECHECK GAY BUCCANEER and CHAMPION FAMECHECK MUSKETEER

Sire Ch. Famecheck Gay Crusader	Ch. Famecheck Happy Knight	Ch. Calluna the Poacher	Calluna Bingo
			Calluna Vermintrude
		Famecheck Fluster	Ch. Barrister of Branston
			Freshney Futurist
	Ch. Famecheck Lucky Charm	Ch. Shiningcliff Sultan	Ch. Melbourne Mathias
			Walney Thistle
		Famecheck Paddy Scalare	Freshney Fatmah
			Freshney Futurist
Dam Ch. Famecheck Lucky Mascot	Ch. Shiningcliff Sultan	Ch. Melbourne Mathias	Ch. Leal Flurry
			Leal Chieftainess
		Walney Thistle	Ch. Wolvey Prefect
			White Sheen of Wick
	Famecheck Paddy Scalare	Freshney Fatmah	Freshney MacRuaridh of Tiriosal
			Freshney Farel
		Freshney Futurist	Freshney Frisk
			Freshney Fairy

CHAMPION PETRIBURG MARK OF POLTEANA

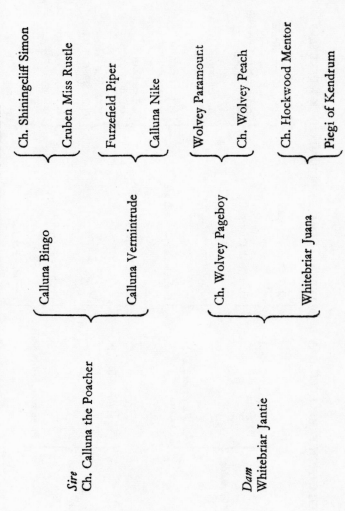

Sire
Ch. Calluna the Poacher

Calluna Bingo
{ Ch. Shiningcliff Simon
  Cruben Miss Rustle

Calluna Vermintrude
{ Furzefield Piper
  Calluna Nike

Dam
Whitebriar Jantie

Ch. Wolvey Pageboy
{ Wolvey Paramount
  Ch. Wolvey Peach

Whitebriar Juana
{ Ch. Hockwood Mentor
  Piegi of Kendrum

WAIDESHOUSE WATERBOY

Sire
Waideshouse Willoughby

- Ch. Petriburg Mark of Polteana
  - Ch. Calluna the Poacher
  - Whitebriar Jantie
- Waideshouse Wickedness
  - Ch. Calluna the Poacher
  - Rowmore Rosette

Dam
Ch. Waideshouse Woodlark

- Waideshouse Wallaby
  - Ch. Kirnbrae Symmetra Sailaway
  - Waideshouse Wistaria
- Waideshouse Wickedness
  - Ch. Calluna the Poacher
  - Rowmore Rosette

CHAMPION QUAKERTOWN QUISTADOR

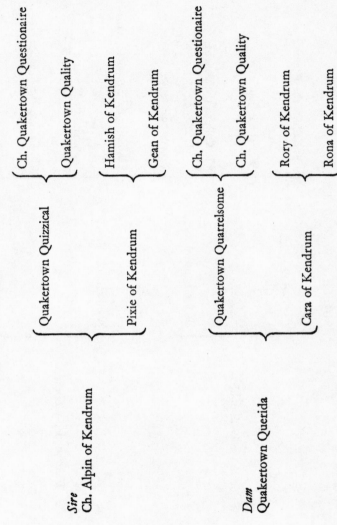

Sire
Ch. Alpin of Kendrum

Quakertown Quizzical
{ Ch. Quakertown Questionaire
  Quakertown Quality

Pixie of Kendrum
{ Hamish of Kendrum
  Gean of Kendrum

Dam
Quakertown Querida

Quakertown Quarrelsome
{ Ch. Quakertown Questionaire
  Ch. Quakertown Quality

Cara of Kendrum
{ Rory of Kendrum
  Rona of Kendrum

CANADIAN CHAMPION HIGHLAND URSA MAJOR

Sire
Belmertle Aldrich

Can. Ch. Robinridge MacBeth
— Eng. & Am. Ch. Ray of Rushmoor
— { Ch. Wolvey Patrician
    Binny of Rushmoor
— Edgerstoune Rarity
— { Clint Courtier
    Clint Creena

Can. Ch. Robinridge Cherie
— Am. Ch. Edgerstoune Roughy
— { Eng. & Am. Ch. Ray of Rushmoor
    Can. Ch. Clint Casserole
— Am. Ch. Wolvey Pace of Edgerstoune
— { Ch. Wolvey Patrician
    Wolvey Promise

Dam
Edgerstoune Stardust

Am. Ch. Edgerstoune Roughy
— Eng. & Am. Ch. Ray of Rushmoor
— { Ch. Wolvey Patrician
    Binny of Rushmoor
— Can. Ch. Clint Casserole
— { Ch. Clint Cocktail
    Clint Caltha

Am. Ch. Edgerstoune Starlet
— Am. Ch. Edgerstoune Royalty
— { Wolvey Phantom of Edgerstoune
    Edgerstoune Raith
— Edgerstoune Joyce
— { Am. Ch. Wolvey Prophet of Edgerstoune
    Can. Ch. Clint Casserole

CHAMPION CALLUNA THE POACHER

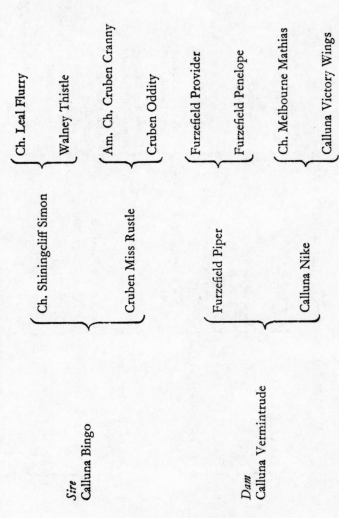

Sire
Calluna Bingo

Ch. Shiningcliff Simon
{
Ch. Leal Flurry
Walney Thistle
}

Cruben Miss Rustle
{
Am. Ch. Cruben Cranny
Cruben Oddity
}

Dam
Calluna Vermintrude

Furzefield Piper
{
Furzefield Provider
Furzefield Penelope
}

Calluna Nike
{
Ch. Melbourne Mathias
Calluna Victory Wings
}

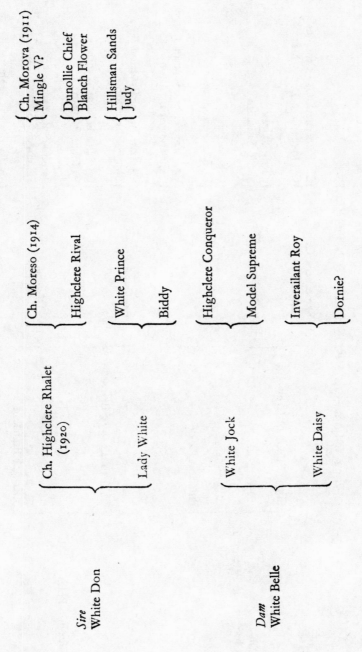

CHAMPION WHITE SYLPH (BITCH) 1920

Sire
White Don
  { Ch. Highclere Rhalet (1920)
    { Ch. Moreso (1914)
        { Ch. Morova (1911)
          Mingle V?
      Highclere Rival
        { Dunollie Chief
          Blanch Flower
  Lady White
    { White Prince
        { Hillsman Sands
          Judy
      Biddy

Dam
White Belle
  { White Jock
    { Highclere Conqueror
      Model Supreme
  White Daisy
    { Inverailant Roy
      Dornie?

163

Eng. and Am.: CHAMPION PILLERTON PETERKIN

Sire
Ch. Pillerton Peterman

- Slitrig Simon of Lynwood
  - Ch. Famecheck Gay Buccaneer
    - Ch. Famecheck Gay Crusader
    - Ch. Famecheck Lucky Mascot
  - Slitrig Sweet Suzette
    - Slitrig Skipper
    - Slitrig Sapphire
- Pillerton Pickle
  - Ch. Calluna The Poacher
    - Calluna Bingo
    - Calluna Vermintrude
  - Blainy of Branston
    - Ch. Nice Fella of Wynsolot
    - Ch. Banda of Branston

Dam
Pillerton Polka

- Ch. Bandsman of Branston
  - Ch. Banker of Branston
    - Ch. Barrister of Branston
    - Binty of Branston
  - Ch. Banessa of Branston
    - Ch. Nice Fella of Wynsolot
    - Baffin of Branston
- Blainy of Branston
  - Ch. Nice Fella of Wynsolot
    - Fan Mail of Wynsolot
    - Shiningcliff Starturn
  - Ch. Banda of Branston
    - Ch. Barrister of Branston
    - Binty of Branston

CHAMPION RHIANFA TAKE NOTICE

Sire
Am. Ch. Lymehills
Birkfell South Pacific

- Eng. & Am. Ch. MacNab of Balmaha
  - Lymehills Rhianfa Viking
    - Ch. Sollershott Soloist
    - Cotsmoor Crackling
  - Pinkholme Prestige
    - Ch. Glengyle Trader
    - Pinkholme Promise
- Ch. Birkfell Solace
  - Ch. Pillerton Peterman
    - Slitrig Simon of Lynwood
    - Pillerton Pickle
  - Ch. Birkfell Solitaire
    - Ch. Famecheck Jolly Roger
    - Birkfell Snowstorm

Dam
Rhianfa Lady Constance
of Estcoss

- Estcoss Beaucaire of Greenlodge
  - Ch. Citrus Lochinvar of Estcoss
    - Ch. Sollershott Sun-up
    - Famecheck Foxtrot
  - Famecheck Vivacious
    - Ch. Famecheck Gay Crusader
    - Ch. Famecheck Lucky Charm
- Ch. Rhianfa Up and Coming of Estcoss
  - Ch. Citrus Lochinvar of Estcoss
    - Ch. Sollershott Sun-Up
    - Famecheck Foxtrot
  - Rianfa Rainsborowe Poppea
    - Ch. Bandsman of Branston
    - Rainsborowe Michala

APPENDIX VI

REGISTRATIONS FROM 1907

1907—141	1931— 540	1953— 895
1908—249	1932— 590	1954— 948
1909—351	1933— 598	1955—1080
1910—442	1934— 628	1956—1327
1911—583	1935— 718	1957—1263
1912—596	1936— 757	1958—1448
1913—631	1937— 682	1959—1785
1914—522	1938— 633	1960—2070
1915—239	1939— 424	1961—2344
1916—193	1940— 138	1962—2614
1917— 97	1941— 135	1963—2744
1918— 55	1942— 175	1964—2884
1919—126	1943— 277	1965—3113
1920—244	1944— 494	1966—3094
1921—371	1945— 675	1967—3611
1922—499	1946—1017	1968—4160
1923—587	1947—1056	1969—4837
1924—688	1948—1114	1970—4933
1925—758	1949—1193	1971—4097
1926—721	1950—1018	1972—4510
1927—715	1951— 992	1973—4472
1928—726	1952— 968	1974—4630
1929—663		
1930—639		

Index